William Sieghart founded the Forward Poetry Prizes in 1992 and National Poetry Day in 1994: both are run by Forward Arts Foundation, an arts charity which celebrates excellence in poetry and brings it to a wide audience through the annual *Forward Book of Poetry* and other initiatives. He has edited two collections of *Poems of the Decade* (2001 and 2011), anthologies featuring the best poems from the Forward Prizes. In 2014, he was commissioned by the government to review the public library service in England.

WINNING WORDS

Inspiring Poems for Everyday Life

chosen and introduced by
William Sieghart

**Forward
Arts
Foundation**

ff

FABER & FABER

First published in 2012
by Faber & Faber Ltd
Bloomsbury House
74–77 Great Russell Street
London WC1B 3DA
and
Forward Arts Foundation
Somerset House
Strand
London WC2R 1LA

This paperback edition first published in 2015

Typeset by RefineCatch Limited, Bungay, Suffolk
Printed in England by CPI Group (UK) Ltd, Croydon, CR0 4YY

A CIP record for this book
is available from the British Library

ISBN 978–0–571–32570–2

FSC
www.fsc.org
MIX
Paper from
responsible sources
FSC® C101712

2 4 6 8 10 9 7 5 3 1

to Molly Dineen with love and thanks

CONTENTS

Foreword by Sebastian Faulks xiii
Introduction by William Sieghart xv

ANON 'I saw a Peacock with a fiery tail' 3
SHEENAGH PUGH What If This Road 4
JOHN KEATS Lines *from* Endymion 5
CHRISTOPHER LOGUE Come to the Edge 6
JOHN GILLESPIE MAGEE High Flight (An Airman's Ecstasy) 7
MAYA ANGELOU Still I Rise 8
GERARD MANLEY HOPKINS Pied Beauty 10
SEAMUS HEANEY The Peninsula 11
WILLIAM WORDSWORTH Upon Westminster Bridge 12
ANNA AKHMATOVA Our Own Land 13
ALFRED, LORD TENNYSON *from* In Memoriam A. H. H. 14
OSCAR HAMMERSTEIN II You'll Never Walk Alone 15
THE KING JAMES BIBLE *from* The Song of Solomon 16
A. A. MILNE The End 17
THOM GUNN The Hug 18
SUSAN COOLIDGE New Every Morning 19
JOHN DONNE *from* Devotions Upon Emergent Occasions 20
ELEANOR FARJEON 'Morning has broken' 21
WILLIAM SHAKESPEARE *from* The Tempest 22
JOHN BURNSIDE History 23
W. B. YEATS The Song of Wandering Aengus 26
WILLIAM BLAKE Eternity 27
CALLIMACHUS Heraclitus 28
JAMES FENTON Hinterhof 29
ROBERT BROWNING Home-Thoughts, from Abroad 30
ANN SANSOM Voice 31

ROBERT HERRICK His Desire 32
WILLIAM CARLOS WILLIAMS Iris 33
PAT BORAN Waving 34
RUPERT BROOKE The Soldier 36
WENDY COPE Being Boring 37
ROBERT BURNS Auld Lang Syne 38
MICHAEL DONAGHY Machines 40
CHRISTOPHER MARLOWE *from* Ovid's Elegies 41
HAFEZ My Brilliant Image 42
T. S. ELIOT The Love Song of J. Alfred Prufrock 43
WALTER D. WINTLE Thinking 49
CHRISTINA ROSSETTI Up-Hill 50
WILLIAM BLAKE *from* Auguries of Innocence 51
SEAN O'BRIEN Dignified 52
ROBERT BROWNING Pippa's Song 54
DYLAN THOMAS And death shall have no dominion 55
JOHN BETJEMAN Seaside Golf 56
ARCHILOCHUS 'Some Saian sports my splendid shield' 57
WILLIAM ERNEST HENLEY Invictus 58
STEPHEN DUNN Happiness 59
WILLIAM BLAKE *from* Milton 60
ADRIAN MITCHELL Celia Celia 61
THEODORE ROETHKE The Waking 62
W. B. YEATS He Wishes for the Cloths of Heaven 63
ROBERT BLY Watering the Horse 64
ELIZABETH BARRETT BROWNING *from* Sonnets from
     the Portuguese 65
WILLIAM WORDSWORTH My Heart Leaps Up 66
DON PATERSON Being 67
ROBERT FROST The Road Not Taken 68
EMILY DICKINSON 'If I can stop one Heart from breaking' 69
EDMUND BLUNDEN Report on Experience 70
STEVIE SMITH Conviction 71

CHRISTINA ROSSETTI A Christmas Carol 72

J. R. R. TOLKIEN 'All that is gold does not glitter' 74

ELIZABETH BISHOP One Art 75

JOHN MASEFIELD An Epilogue 76

THOMAS HARDY Afterwards 77

WILLIAM SHAKESPEARE *from* Henry V 78

CLARE POLLARD Thinking of England 80

ELLA WHEELER WILCOX Solitude 85

DOROTHY PARKER Penelope 86

ALICE OSWALD Wedding 87

ROBERT GRAVES Warning to Children 88

GEORGE HERBERT Prayer 90

SEAMUS HEANEY *from* Markings 91

A. E. HOUSMAN *from* A Shropshire Lad 92

WENDY COPE Two Cures for Love 93

JOHN DRYDEN Happy the Man 94

SIEGFRIED SASSOON Everyone Sang 95

SHMUEL HANAGID Soar, Don't Settle 96

LANGSTON HUGHES I, Too 97

JOHN KEATS On First Looking into Chapman's Homer 98

ROBERT HERRICK The End 99

AMY LOWELL Climbing 100

WILLIAM SHAKESPEARE *from* Richard II 101

MARIANNE MOORE I May, I Might, I Must 102

MAURA DOOLEY Freight 103

RUDYARD KIPLING If – 104

PASTOR NIEMÖLLER 'First they came for the Jews' 106

CHARLES CAUSLEY I Am the Song 107

KATHLEEN JAMIE The Way We Live 108

ROBERT FROST Riders 109

COLETTE BRYCE Early Version 110

ALFRED, LORD TENNYSON The Charge of the Light Brigade 111

SIMON ARMITAGE 'Let me put it this way' 114

[ix]

W. B. YEATS An Irish Airman Foresees His Death 115

SHEENAGH PUGH Envying Owen Beattie 116

WALTER DE LA MARE Fare Well 118

WALT WHITMAN 'We two boys together clinging' 119

LEONARDO DA VINCI 'He turns not back who is bound
to a star' 120

JALALUDDIN RUMI 'Come, come, for you will not find
another friend like Me' 121

ROGER MCGOUGH The Way Things Are 122

MARY E. FRYE 'Do not stand at my grave and weep' 124

MAYA ANGELOU I Know Why the Caged Bird Sings 125

MATTHEW ARNOLD Dover Beach 127

U. A. FANTHORPE Atlas 129

ANON Life's Variety 130

WILLIAM BLAKE 'The Angel that presided o'er my birth' 131

W. H. AUDEN 'As I walked out one evening' 132

JOHN CLARE 'I Am' 135

WILLIAM WORDSWORTH The Daffodils 136

ANNE BRADSTREET To my Dear and Loving Husband 137

PABLO NERUDA Dead Woman 138

JACKIE KAY Holy Island 140

ANDREW MARVELL *from* Thoughts in a Garden 141

PHILIP LARKIN The Trees 142

DEREK MAHON Everything is Going to Be All Right 143

PERCY BYSSHE SHELLEY *from* Prometheus Unbound 144

EDWARD THOMAS Adlestrop 145

SIR HENRY WOTTON The Character of a Happy Life 146

E. E. CUMMINGS 'i thank You God for most this amazing' 148

GEOFFREY CHAUCER Roundel 149

WILLIAM HENRY DAVIES Leisure 150

CAROL ANN DUFFY Talent 151

GEORGE ELIOT Count That Day Lost 152

LOUIS MACNEICE Apple Blossom 153

CRAIG RAINE Heaven on Earth 154

CHRISTOPHER MARLOWE The Passionate Shepherd to
his Love 155

DENISE LEVERTOV Variation on a Theme by Rilke 157

TED HUGHES Full Moon and Little Frieda 158

GERARD MANLEY HOPKINS Spring 159

SEAMUS HEANEY The Railway Children 160

CHARLES SIMIC The Old World 161

JAMES WRIGHT Lying in a Hammock at William Duffy's Farm
in Pine Island, Minnesota 162

SYLVIA PLATH You're 163

ALISON FELL Pushing Forty 164

ARTHUR HUGH CLOUGH 'Say not the struggle nought
availeth' 165

LOUIS UNTERMEYER Portrait of a Child 166

JOHN DONNE The Good Morrow 167

WENDELL BERRY The Peace of Wild Things 168

DYLAN THOMAS Do not go gentle into that good night 169

DOUGLAS DUNN Modern Love 170

JOHN MILTON On His Blindness 171

OGDEN NASH Reflections on Ice-Breaking 172

PHILIP LARKIN Church Going 173

SIMONIDES For the Spartan Dead at Thermopylai 176

EMILY BRONTË The Old Stoic 177

DEREK WALCOTT Earth 178

ROBERT HERRICK To the Virgins, to Make Much of Time 179

GAVIN EWART June 1966 180

W. H. AUDEN 'Some say that love's a little boy' 181

SIMON ARMITAGE The Catch 183

RAYMOND CARVER Happiness 184

PATRICK KAVANAGH Inniskeen Road: July Evening 185

GEORGE GORDON, LORD BYRON She Walks in Beauty 186

LANGSTON HUGHES Dreams 187

D. H. LAWRENCE Green 188
CHRISTINA ROSSETTI A Birthday 189
MICHAEL DONAGHY The Present 190
ANON 'What I spent I had' 191
SAMUEL TAYLOR COLERIDGE Frost at Midnight 192
RAYMOND CARVER Late Fragment 195
T. S. ELIOT *from* Little Gidding 196

Acknowledgements 199
Index of Poets 205
Index of Titles and First Lines 207

FOREWORD

Literature began with poetry and will doubtless one day end with it. For all the efforts of Tolstoy, Dickens and Proust, it is the short lines of the poets that speak most directly to their readers; it is they who touch what is both primitive and noble in us.

You know when it has happened: when the significance of a line or stanza outweighs the sum of the words involved; when you see that no syllable could be moved or changed; when you have the sense that the poet has revealed to us something which – in some mysterious way – already existed.

It is a joy to partake in such transcendence; we are inspired by it. And the poems in this anthology celebrate a sense of inspiration. The book grew from a search for some lines to be reproduced on the walls of the Olympic village in the London Games in 2012. The lines finally chosen – from the conclusion of Tennyson's 'Ulysses' – speak of the nobility of striving to explore, to do one's best, even in the shadow of death. This idea lies behind many of the most uplifting poems here as well as the more humorous, such as Sean O'Brien's 'Dignified'. What can we poor humans do when we know that all is ultimately futile? Run faster, jump higher, laugh louder . . . Make better verses. And the sporting poems here are not all about record-breakers; John Betjeman's 'Seaside Golf' records the moment at which a high handicapper can look Jack Nicklaus in the face with his 'quite unprecedented three'.

The scope of this book has been widened from the simply athletic. Philip Larkin's 'The Trees' finds its inspiration in the most repetitive of natural processes – though the words in which it does so are far from predictable: 'The trees are coming into leaf/Like something almost being said'. The Persian poet Hafez shows in his little poem 'My Brilliant Image' how one man's vision can be used to inspire another.

The old favourites here repay another reading; the less familiar are worth getting to know. Each in its way reflects the glorious futility of living, though each manages to find a way to stress the glory over the futility – none more than Alfred, Lord Tennyson:

> that which we are, we are;
> One equal temper of heroic hearts,
> Made weak by time and fate, but strong in will
> To strive, to seek, to find and not to yield.

SEBASTIAN FAULKS

Spring 2012

INTRODUCTION

This anthology was inspired by the arrival of the Olympic Games in London in the summer of 2012. Searching for a genuine cultural legacy for this finite sporting event, I set about creating a partnership with the Games' organisers, to ensure the place of poetry in the physical infrastructure of the Olympic venues and to encourage people across Britain to put poetry into the landscape around them as a celebration of the events of 2012.

Poetry and the English language are our great cultural legacies. The writings of Shakespeare and Chaucer and countless others are treasured the world over. Poetry has also a unique place in the hearts of the British people. Whether it is found in the slim volumes of verse in the back of a bookshop or library, the lyrics of songs or hymns, the chants on the football terraces, the words in greetings cards or jingles on the radio, poetry plays a daily role in our lives.

This is an unashamedly personal selection that uses the word 'inspiring' as its criteria for selection in its broadest sense. I hope, like all good anthologies, *Winning Words* will work for both the dedicated and occasional reader; a book to sit by the bedside for inspiration and reflection. Many people turn to poetry in times of need, to find complicity with how they feel but don't necessarily have the language to express themselves. I hope the reader will find poetry here for all moods, poetry that will give hope, understanding and inspiration to help get them through the trials and tribulations of everyday life.

I would like to thank some key co-conspirators in this project: Wynn Weldon who tirelessly searched through archives for me to find me poems I never knew existed, and Rachel

Alexander, Hannah Griffiths, Matthew Hollis and Anne Owen at Faber and Faber, and of course Sebastian Faulks who generously offered a Foreword.

Most of all I would like to thank poetry itself for giving me a lifetime of pleasure, companionship and support.

WILLIAM SIEGHART
Spring 2012

WINNING WORDS

ANON

I saw a Peacock with a fiery tail
I saw a blazing Comet drop down hail
I saw a Cloud with Ivy circled round
I saw a sturdy Oak creep on the ground
I saw a Pismire swallow up a Whale
I saw a raging Sea brim full of Ale
I saw a Venice Glass sixteen foot deep
I saw a Well full of men's tears that weep
I saw their Eyes all in a flame of fire
I saw a House as big as the Moon and higher
I saw the Sun even in the midst of night
I saw the Man that saw this wondrous sight.

17th century

SHEENAGH PUGH

What If This Road

What if this road, that has held no surprises
these many years, decided not to go
home after all; what if it could turn
left or right with no more ado
than a kite-tail? What if its tarry skin
were like a long, supple bolt of cloth,
that is shaken and rolled out, and takes
a new shape from the contours beneath?
And if it chose to lay itself down
in a new way; around a blind corner,
across hills you must climb without knowing
what's on the other side; who would not hanker
to be going, at all risks? Who wants to know
a story's end, or where a road will go?

JOHN KEATS

Lines *from* Endymion

A thing of beauty is a joy for ever:
Its loveliness increases; it will never
Pass into nothingness; but still will keep
A bower quiet for us, and a sleep
Full of sweet dreams, and health, and quiet breathing.
Therefore, on every morrow, are we wreathing
A flowery band to bind us to the earth,
Spite of despondence, of the inhuman dearth
Of noble natures, of the gloomy days,
Of all the unhealthy and o'er-darkened ways
Made for our searching: yes, in spite of all,
Some shape of beauty moves away the pall
From our dark spirits.

CHRISTOPHER LOGUE

Come to the Edge

Come to the edge.
We might fall.
Come to the edge.
It's too high!
COME TO THE EDGE!
And they came,
And he pushed,
And they flew.

JOHN GILLESPIE MAGEE

High Flight (An Airman's Ecstasy)

Oh, I have slipped the surly bonds of earth
And danced the skies on laughter-silvered wings;
Sunward I've climbed and joined the tumbling mirth
Of sun-split clouds – and done a hundred things
You have not dreamed of; wheeled and soared and swung
High in the sun-lit silence. Hovering there
I've chased the shouting wind along, and flung
My eager craft through footless halls of air;
Up, up the long, delirious, burning blue
I've topped the wind-swept heights with easy grace,
Where never lark nor even eagle flew;
And while, with silent lifting mind I've trod
The high untrespassed sanctity of space,
Put out my hand, and touched the face of God.

MAYA ANGELOU

Still I Rise

You may write me down in history
With your bitter, twisted lies,
You may trod me in the very dirt
But still, like dust, I'll rise.

Does my sassiness upset you?
Why are you beset with gloom?
'Cause I walk like I've got oil wells
Pumping in my living room.

Just like moons and like suns,
With the certainty of tides,
Just like hopes springing high,
Still I'll rise.

Did you want to see me broken?
Bowed head and lowered eyes?
Shoulders falling down like teardrops,
Weakened by my soulful cries.

Does my haughtiness offend you?
Don't you take it awful hard
'Cause I laugh like I've got gold mines
Diggin' in my own back yard.

You may shoot me with your words,
You may cut me with your eyes,
You may kill me with your hatefulness,
But still, like air, I'll rise.

Does my sexiness upset you?
Does it come as a surprise
That I dance like I've got diamonds
At the meeting of my thighs?

Out of the huts of history's shame
I rise
Up from a past that's rooted in pain
I rise
I'm a black ocean, leaping and wide,
Welling and swelling I bear in the tide.

Leaving behind nights of terror and fear
I rise
Into a daybreak that's wondrously clear
I rise
Bringing the gifts that my ancestors gave,
I am the dream and the hope of the slave.
I rise
I rise
I rise.

GERARD MANLEY HOPKINS

Pied Beauty

Glory be to God for dappled things –
  For skies of couple-colour as a brinded cow;
    For rose-moles all in stipple upon trout that swim;
Fresh-firecoal chestnut-falls; finches' wings;
  Landscape plotted and pieced – fold, fallow, and plough;
    And áll trádes, their gear and tackle and trim.

All things counter, original, spare, strange;
  Whatever is fickle, freckled (who knows how?)
    With swift, slow; sweet, sour; adazzle, dim;
He fathers-forth whose beauty is past change:
        Praise him.

SEAMUS HEANEY

The Peninsula

When you have nothing more to say, just drive
For a day all round the peninsula.
The sky is tall as over a runway,
The land without marks, so you will not arrive

But pass through, though always skirting landfall.
At dusk, horizons drink down sea and hill,
The ploughed field swallows the whitewashed gable
And you're in the dark again. Now recall

The glazed foreshore and silhouetted log,
That rock where breakers shredded into rags,
The leggy birds stilted on their own legs,
Islands riding themselves out into the fog,

And drive back home, still with nothing to say
Except that now you will uncode all landscapes
By this: things founded clean on their own shapes,
Water and ground in their extremity.

WILLIAM WORDSWORTH

Upon Westminster Bridge

3 Sept, 1802

Earth has not anything to show more fair:
Dull would he be of soul who could pass by
A sight so touching in its majesty:
This City now doth like a garment wear

The beauty of the morning: silent, bare,
Ships, towers, domes, theatres, and temples lie
Open unto the fields, and to the sky,
All bright and glittering in the smokeless air.

Never did sun more beautifully steep
In his first splendour valley, rock, or hill;
Ne'er saw I, never felt, a calm so deep!

The river glideth at his own sweet will:
Dear God! the very houses seem asleep;
And all that mighty heart is lying still!

ANNA AKHMATOVA

Our Own Land

There is no one in the world more tearless,
more proud, more simple than us.

1922

We don't wear it in sacred amulets on our chests.
We don't compose hysterical poems about it.
It does not disturb our bitter dream-sleep.
It doesn't seem to be the promised paradise.
We don't make of it a soul
object for sale and barter,
and we being sick, poverty-stricken, unable to utter a word
don't even remember about it.
Yes, for us it's mud on galoshes,
   for us it's crunch on teeth,
   and we mill, mess and crush
   that dust and ashes
   that is not mixed up in anything.
But we'll lie in it and be it,
that's why, so freely, we call it our own.

Leningrad, 1961
translated from the Russian by Richard McKane

ALFRED, LORD TENNYSON

from In Memoriam A. H. H.

XXVII

I envy not in any moods
   The captive void of noble rage,
   The linnet born within the cage,
That never knew the summer woods:

I envy not the beast that takes
   His license in the field of time,
   Unfettered by the sense of crime,
To whom a conscience never wakes;

Nor, what may count itself as blest,
   The heart that never plighted troth
   But stagnates in the weeds of sloth;
Nor any want-begotten rest.

I hold it true, whate'er befall;
   I feel it, when I sorrow most;
   'Tis better to have loved and lost
Than never to have loved at all.

OSCAR HAMMERSTEIN II

You'll Never Walk Alone

Walk on, through the wind
Walk on, through the rain
Though your dreams be tossed and blown
Walk on, walk on, with hope in your heart
And you'll never walk alone
You'll never walk alone

THE KING JAMES BIBLE

from The Song of Solomon

My beloved spake, and said unto me, Rise up,
   my love, my fair one, and come away.
For lo, the winter is past, the rain is over, and gone.
The flowers appear on the earth, the time of the
   singing of birds is come, and the voice of the
   turtle is heard in our land.
The fig tree putteth forth her green figs, and the
   vines with the tender grape give a good smell.
Arise, my love, my fair one, and come away.

The End

When I was One,
I had just begun.

When I was Two,
I was nearly new.

When I was Three,
I was hardly Me.

When I was Four,
I was not much more.

When I was Five,
I was just alive.

But now I am Six, I'm as clever as clever.
So I think I'll be six now for ever and ever.

THOM GUNN

The Hug

It was your birthday, we had drunk and dined
      Half of the night with our old friend
         Who'd showed us in the end
      To a bed I reached in one drunk stride.
         Already I lay snug,
And drowsy with the wine dozed on one side.

I dozed, I slept. My sleep broke on a hug,
      Suddenly, from behind,
In which the full lengths of our bodies pressed:
      Your instep to my heel,
   My shoulder-blades against your chest.
   It was not sex, but I could feel
   The whole strength of your body set,
         Or braced, to mine,
      And locking me to you
   As if we were still twenty-two
   When our grand passion had not yet
      Become familial.
   My quick sleep had deleted all
   Of intervening time and place.
         I only knew
The stay of your secure firm dry embrace.

[18]

SUSAN COOLIDGE

New Every Morning

Every day is a fresh beginning,
Listen my soul to the glad refrain.
    And, spite of old sorrows
        And older sinning,
        Troubles forecasted
        And possible pain,
Take heart with the day and begin again.

JOHN DONNE

from Devotions Upon Emergent Occasions

No Man is an *Island*, entire of it self; every man is a piece of the *Continent*, a part of the *main*; if a *Clod* be washed away by the *Sea*, *Europe* is the less, as well as if a *Promontory* were, as well as if a *Manor* of thy *friends*, or of *thine own* were; Any Man's *death* diminishes *me*, because I am involved in *Mankind*; And therefore never send to know for whom the *bell* tolls; It tolls for *thee*.

ELEANOR FARJEON

Morning has broken
Like the first morning,
Blackbird has spoken
　　Like the first bird.
　　　Praise for the singing!
　　　Praise for the morning!
　　　Praise for them, springing
　　　Fresh from the Word!

Sweet the rain's new fall
Sunlit from heaven,
Like the first dewfall
　　On the first grass.
　　　Praise for the sweetness
　　　Of the wet garden,
　　　Sprung in completeness
　　　Where his feet pass.

Mine is the sunlight!
Mine is the morning
Born of the one light
　　Eden saw play!
　　　Praise with elation,
　　　Praise every morning,
　　　God's re-creation
　　　Of the new day!

WILLIAM SHAKESPEARE

from The Tempest

Act IV, Scene i

Be cheerful, sir:
Our revels now are ended. These our actors,
As I foretold you, were all spirits and
Are melted into air, into thin air:
And, like the baseless fabric of this vision,
The cloud-capp'd towers, the gorgeous palaces,
The solemn temples, the great globe itself,
Yea, all which it inherit, shall dissolve
And, like this insubstantial pageant faded,
Leave not a rack behind. We are such stuff
As dreams are made on, and our little life
Is rounded with a sleep.

JOHN BURNSIDE

History

St Andrews: West Sands; September 2001

Today
        as we flew the kites
– the sand spinning off in ribbons along the beach
and that gasoline smell from Leuchars gusting across
the golf links;
        the tide far out
and quail-grey in the distance;
                                        people
jogging, or stopping to watch
as the war planes cambered and turned
in the morning light –

today
        – with the news in my mind, and the muffled dread
of what may come –

                                I knelt down in the sand
with Lucas
                gathering shells
and pebbles
                        finding evidence of life in all this
driftwork:
                snail shells; shreds of razorfish;
smudges of weed and flesh on tideworn stone.

At times I think what makes us who we are
is neither kinship nor our given states
but something lost between the world we own
and what we dream about behind the names
on days like this
                    our lines raised in the wind
our bodies fixed and anchored to the shore

and though we are confined by property
what tethers us to gravity and light
has most to do with distance and the shapes
we find in water
                    reading from the book
of silt and tides
                    the rose or petrol blue
of jellyfish and sea anemone
combining with a child's
first nakedness.

Sometimes I am dizzy with the fear
of losing everything – the sea, the sky,
all living creatures, forests, estuaries:
we trade so much to know the virtual
we scarcely register the drift and tug
of other bodies
                    scarcely apprehend
the moment as it happens: shifts of light
and weather
                    and the quiet, local forms
of history: the fish lodged in the tide
beyond the sands;
                    the long insomnia

of ornamental carp in public parks
captive and bright
                    and hung in their own
slow-burning
                transitive gold;
                            jamjars of spawn
and sticklebacks
                    or goldfish carried home
from fairgrounds
                    to the hum of radio

but this is the problem: how to be alive
in all this gazed-upon and cherished world
and do no harm

                    a toddler on a beach
sifting wood and dried weed from the sand
and puzzled by the pattern on a shell

his parents on the dune slacks with a kite
plugged into the sky
                        all nerve and line

patient; afraid; but still, through everything
attentive to the irredeemable.

The Song of Wandering Aengus

I went out to the hazel wood,
Because a fire was in my head,
And cut and peeled a hazel wand,
And hooked a berry to a thread;
And when white moths were on the wing,
And moth-like stars were flickering out,
I dropped the berry in a stream
And caught a little silver trout.

When I had laid it on the floor
I went to blow the fire aflame,
But something rustled on the floor,
And some one called me by my name:
It had become a glimmering girl
With apple blossom in her hair
Who called me by my name and ran
And faded through the brightening air.

Though I am old with wandering
Through hollow lands and hilly lands,
I will find out where she has gone,
And kiss her lips and take her hands;
And walk among long dappled grass,
And pluck till time and times are done
The silver apples of the moon,
The golden apples of the sun.

WILLIAM BLAKE

Eternity

He who binds to himself a joy
Does the wingèd life destroy;
But he who kisses the joy as it flies
Lives in eternity's sun rise.

CALLIMACHUS

Heraclitus

They told me, Heraclitus, they told me you were dead;
They brought me bitter news to hear and bitter tears to shed.
I wept as I remembered how often you and I
Had tired the sun with talking and sent him down the sky.

And now that thou art lying, my dear old Carian guest,
A handful of grey ashes, long long ago at rest,
Still are thy pleasant voices, thy nightingales, awake,
For Death, he taketh all away, but them he cannot take.

translated from the Greek by William Johnson Cory

JAMES FENTON

Hinterhof

Stay near to me and I'll stay near to you –
As near as you are dear to me will do,
   Near as the rainbow to the rain,
   The west wind to the windowpane,
As fire to the hearth, as dawn to dew.

Stay true to me and I'll stay true to you –
As true as you are new to me will do,
   New as the rainbow in the spray,
   Utterly new in every way,
New in the way that what you say is true.

Stay near to me, stay true to me. I'll stay
As near, as true to you as heart could pray.
   Heart never hoped that one might be
   Half of the things you are to me –
The dawn, the fire, the rainbow and the day.

ROBERT BROWNING

Home-Thoughts, from Abroad

Oh, to be in England
Now that April's there,
And whoever wakes in England
Sees, some morning, unaware,
That the lowest boughs and the brushwood sheaf
Round the elm-tree bole are in tiny leaf,
While the chaffinch sings on the orchard bough
In England – now!

And after April, when May follows,
And the whitethroat builds, and all the swallows –
Hark! where my blossomed pear-tree in the hedge
Leans to the field and scatters on the clover
Blossoms and dewdrops – at the bent spray's edge –
That's the wise thrush; he sings each song twice over,
Lest you should think he never could recapture
The first fine careless rapture!
And though the fields look rough with hoary dew,
All will be gay when noontide wakes anew
The buttercups, the little children's dower,
– Far brighter than this gaudy melon-flower!

ANN SANSOM

Voice

Call, by all means, but just once
don't use the *broken heart again* voice;
the *I'm sick to death of life and women
and romance* voice *but with a little help
I'll try to struggle on* voice

Spare me the promise and the curse
voice, the ansafoney *Call me, please
when you get in* voice, the *nobody knows
the trouble I've seen* voice; the *I'd value
your advice* voice.

I want the how it was voice;
the *call me irresponsible but aren't I nice* voice;
the *such a bastard but I warn them in advance* voice.
The *We all have weaknesses
and mine is being wicked* voice

the *life's short and wasting time's
the only vice* voice, the *stay in touch,
but out of reach* voice. I want to hear
the *things it's better not to broach* voice
the *things it's wiser not to voice* voice.

ROBERT HERRICK

His Desire

Give me a man that is not dull,
When all the world with rifts is full:
But unamaz'd dares clearely sing,
When as the roof's a tottering:
And, though it falls, continues still
Tickling the Citterne with his quill.

WILLIAM CARLOS WILLIAMS

Iris

a burst of iris so that
come down for
breakfast

we searched through the
rooms for
that

sweetest odor and at
first could not
find its

source then a blue as
of the sea
struck

startling us from among
those trumpeting
petals

Waving

As a child I waved to people I didn't know.
I waved from passing cars, school buses,
second-floor windows, or from the street
to secretaries trapped in offices above.
When policemen motioned my father on
past the scene of the crime or an army checkpoint,
I waved back from the back seat. I loved to wave.
I saw the world disappear into a funnel
of perspective, like the reflection in a bath
sucked into a single point when the water
drains. I waved in greeting at things that vanished
into points. I waved to say, 'I see you: can you see me?'

I loved 'the notion of an ocean' that could wave,
of a sea that rose up to see the onlooker
standing on the beach. And though the sea
came towards the beach, it was a different sea
when it arrived; the onlooker too had changed.
They disappeared, both of them, into points in time.
So that was why they waved to one another.
On the beach I waved until my arms hurt.

My mother waved her hair sometimes. This,
I know, seems to be something else. But,
when she came up the street, bright and radiant,
her white hair like a jewel-cap on her head,
it was a signal I could not fail to answer.
I waved and she approached me, smiling shyly.

Sometimes someone walking beside her
might wave back, wondering where they knew me from.
Hands itched in pockets, muscles twitched
when I waved. 'There's someone who sees me!'
But in general people took no risk with strangers.
And when they saw who I was – or wasn't –
they felt relief, saved from terrible disgrace.

Now it turns out that light itself's a wave
(as well as a point, or points), so though the waving's
done, it's really only just beginning. Whole humans –
arms, legs, backs, bellies – are waving away,
flickering on and off, in and out of time
and space, pushing through streets with heads down,
smiling up at office windows, lying in gutters
with their kneecaps broken and their hopes dashed,
driving, loving, hiding, growing old, and always
waving, waving as if to say: 'Can you see me?
I can see you – still . . . still . . . still . . .'

RUPERT BROOKE

The Soldier

If I should die, think only this of me:
    That there's some corner of a foreign field
That is for ever England. There shall be
    In that rich earth a richer dust concealed;
A dust whom England bore, shaped, made aware,
    Gave, once her flowers to love, her ways to roam,
A body of England's, breathing English air,
    Washed by the rivers, blessed by the suns of home.

And think, this heart, all evil shed away,
    A pulse in the eternal mind, no less
        Gives somewhere back the thoughts by England given;
Her sights and sounds; dreams happy as her day;
    And laughter, learnt of friends; and gentleness,
        In hearts a peace, under an English heaven.

WENDY COPE

Being Boring

'May you live in interesting times.' – Chinese curse

If you ask me 'What's new?', I have nothing to say
Except that the garden is growing.
I had a slight cold but it's better today.
I'm content with the way things are going.
Yes, he is the same as he usually is,
Still eating and sleeping and snoring.
I get on with my work. He gets on with his.
I know this is all very boring.

There was drama enough in my turbulent past:
Tears and passion – I've used up a tankful.
No news is good news, and long may it last.
If nothing much happens, I'm thankful.
A happier cabbage you never did see,
My vegetable spirits are soaring.
If you're after excitement, steer well clear of me.
I want to go on being boring.

I don't go to parties. Well, what are they for,
If you don't need to find a new lover?
You drink and you listen and drink a bit more
And you take the next day to recover.
Someone to stay home with was all my desire
And, now that I've found a safe mooring,
I've just one ambition in life: I aspire
To go on and on being boring.

ROBERT BURNS

Auld Lang Syne

Should auld acquaintance be forgot,
   And never brought to min'?
Should auld acquaintance be forgot,
   And auld lang syne?

For auld lang syne, my dear.
   For auld lang syne,
We'll tak a cup o' kindness yet,
   For auld lang syne.

We twa hae run about the braes,
   And pu'd the gowans fine;
But we've wandered mony a weary foot
   Sin' auld lang syne.

We twa hae paidled i' the burn,
   From morning sun till dine;
But seas between us braid hae roared
   Sin' auld lang syne.

And there's a hand, my trusty fiere,
   And gie's a hand o' thine;
And we'll tak a right guid-willie waught,
   For auld lang syne.

And surely ye'll be your pint-stowp,
   And surely I'll be mine;
And we'll tak a cup o' kindness yet
   For auld lang syne.

MICHAEL DONAGHY

Machines

Dearest, note how these two are alike:
This harpsichord pavane by Purcell
And the racer's twelve-speed bike.

The machinery of grace is always simple.
This chrome trapezoid, one wheel connected
To another of concentric gears,
Which Ptolemy dreamt of and Schwinn perfected,
Is gone. The cyclist, not the cycle, steers.
And in the playing, Purcell's chords are played away.

So this talk, or touch if I were there,
Should work its effortless gadgetry of love,
Like Dante's heaven, and melt into the air.

If it doesn't, of course, I've fallen. So much is chance,
So much agility, desire, and feverish care,
As bicyclists and harpsichordists prove

Who only by moving can balance,
Only by balancing move.

CHRISTOPHER MARLOWE

from Ovid's Elegies, Book I: Elegia V

Corinnae concubitus

In summer's heat, and mid-time of the day,
To rest my limbs upon a bed I lay;
One window shut, the other open stood,
Which gave such light as twinkles in a wood,
Like twilight glimpse at setting of the sun,
Or night being past, and yet not day begun.
Such light to shamefast maidens must be shown,
Where they may sport and seem to be unknown.
Then came Corinna in a long loose gown,
Her white neck hid with tresses hanging down,
Resembling fair Semiramis going to bed,
Or Lais of a thousand wooers sped.
I snatched her gown; being thin, the harm was small,
Yet strived she to be covered therewithal,
And striving thus as one that would be cast,
Betrayed herself, and yielded at the last.
Stark naked as she stood before mine eye,
Not one wen in her body could I spy.
What arms and shoulders did I touch and see,
How apt her breasts were to be pressed by me!
How smooth a belly under her waist saw I,
How large a leg, and what a lusty thigh!
To leave the rest, all liked me passing well;
I clinged her naked body, down she fell.
Judge you the rest: being tired she bade me kiss;
Jove send me more such afternoons as this.

HAFEZ

My Brilliant Image

I wish I could show you
When you are lonely or in darkness,

The Astonishing Light
Of your own Being!

T. S. ELIOT

The Love Song of J. Alfred Prufrock

S'io credessi che mia risposta fosse
a persona che mai tornasse al mondo,
questa fiamma staria senza più scosse.
Ma per ciò che giammai di questo fondo
non tornò vivo alcun, s'i'odo il vero,
senza terna d'infamia ti rispondo.

Let us go then, you and I,
When the evening is spread out against the sky
Like a patient etherised upon a table;
Let us go, through certain half-deserted streets,
The muttering retreats
Of restless nights in one-night cheap hotels
And sawdust restaurants with oyster-shells:
Streets that follow like a tedious argument
Of insidious intent
To lead you to an overwhelming question . . .
Oh, do not ask, 'What is it?'
Let us go and make our visit.

In the room the women come and go
Talking of Michelangelo.

The yellow fog that rubs its back upon the window-panes,
The yellow smoke that rubs its muzzle on the window-panes,
Licked its tongue into the corners of the evening,
Lingered upon the pools that stand in drains,

Let fall upon its back the soot that falls from chimneys,
Slipped by the terrace, made a sudden leap,
And seeing that it was a soft October night,
Curled once about the house, and fell asleep.

And indeed there will be time
For the yellow smoke that slides along the street
Rubbing its back upon the window-panes;
There will be time, there will be time
To prepare a face to meet the faces that you meet;
There will be time to murder and create,
And time for all the works and days of hands
That lift and drop a question on your plate;
Time for you and time for me,
And time yet for a hundred indecisions,
And for a hundred visions and revisions,
Before the taking of a toast and tea.

In the room the women come and go
Talking of Michelangelo.

And indeed there will be time
To wonder, 'Do I dare?' and, 'Do I dare?'
Time to turn back and descend the stair,
With a bald spot in the middle of my hair –
(They will say: 'How his hair is growing thin!')
My morning coat, my collar mounting firmly to the chin,
My necktie rich and modest, but asserted by a simple pin –
(They will say: 'But how his arms and legs are thin!')
Do I dare
Disturb the universe?
In a minute there is time
For decisions and revisions which a minute will reverse.

For I have known them all already, known them all –
Have known the evenings, mornings, afternoons,
I have measured out my life with coffee spoons;
I know the voices dying with a dying fall
Beneath the music from a farther room.
  So how should I presume?

And I have known the eyes already, known them all –
The eyes that fix you in a formulated phrase,
And when I am formulated, sprawling on a pin,
When I am pinned and wriggling on the wall,
Then how should I begin
To spit out all the butt-ends of my days and ways?
  And how should I presume?

And I have known the arms already, known them all –
Arms that are braceleted and white and bare
(But in the lamplight, downed with light brown hair!)
Is it perfume from a dress
That makes me so digress?
Arms that lie along a table, or wrap about a shawl.
  And should I then presume?
  And how should I begin?

        .   .   .   .   .

Shall I say, I have gone at dusk through narrow streets
And watched the smoke that rises from the pipes
Of lonely men in shirt-sleeves, leaning out of windows? . . .

I should have been a pair of ragged claws
Scuttling across the floors of silent seas.

        .   .   .   .   .

And the afternoons, the evening, sleeps so peacefully!
Smoothed by long fingers,
Asleep ... tired ... or it malingers,
Stretched on the floor, here beside you and me.
Should I, after tea and cakes and ices,
Have the strength to force the moment to its crisis?
But though I have wept and fasted, wept and prayed,
Though I have seen my head (grown slightly bald)
    brought in upon a platter,
I am no prophet – and here's no great matter;
I have seen the moment of my greatness flicker,
and I have seen the eternal Footman hold my coat, and snicker,
And in short, I was afraid.

    And would it have been worth it, after all,
After the cups, the marmalade, the tea,
Among the porcelain, among some talk of you and me,
Would it have been worth while,
To have bitten off the matter with a smile,
To have squeezed the universe into a ball
To roll it towards some overwhelming question,
To say: 'I am Lazarus, come from the dead,
Come back to tell you all, I shall tell you all' –
If one, settling a pillow by her head,
    Should say: 'That is not what I meant at all.
    That is not it, at all.'

    And would it have been worth it, after all,
Would it have been worth while,
After the sunsets and the dooryards and the sprinkled
    streets,
After the novels, after the teacups, after the skirts that
    trail along the floor –

And this, and so much more? –
It is impossible to say just what I mean!
But as if a magic lantern threw the nerves in patterns on a
    screen:
Would it have been worth while
If one, settling a pillow or throwing off a shawl,
And turning toward the window, should say:
    'That is not it at all,
     That is not what I meant at all.'

.   .   .   .   .

    No! I am not Prince Hamlet, nor was meant to be;
Am an attendant lord, one that will do
To swell a progress, start a scene or two,
Advise the prince; no doubt, an easy tool,
Deferential, glad to be of use,
Politic, cautious, and meticulous;
Full of high sentence, but a bit obtuse;
At times, indeed, almost ridiculous –
Almost, at times, the Fool.

    I grow old . . . I grow old . . .
I shall wear the bottoms of my trousers rolled.

    Shall I part my hair behind? Do I dare eat a peach?
I shall wear white flannel trousers, and walk upon the beach.
I have heard the mermaids singing, each to each.

I do not think that they will sing to me.

I have seen them riding seaward on the waves
Combing the white hair of the waves blown back
When the wind blows the water white and black.

We have lingered in the chambers of the sea
By sea-girls wreathed with seaweed red and brown
Till human voices wake us, and we drown.

WALTER D. WINTLE

Thinking

If you think you are beaten, you are.
If you think you dare not, you don't.
If you like to win but think you can't,
It's almost a cinch you won't.
If you think you'll lose, you're lost.
For out in the world we find
Success begins with a fellow's will.
It's all in the state of mind.
If you think you are out classed, you are.
You've got to think high to rise.
You've got to be sure of your-self before
You can ever win the prize.
Life's battles don't always go
To the stronger or faster man.
But sooner or later, the man who wins
Is the man who thinks he can.

CHRISTINA ROSSETTI

Up-Hill

Does the road wind up-hill all the way?
   Yes, to the very end.
Will the day's journey take the whole long day?
   From morn to night, my friend.

But is there for the night a resting-place?
   A roof for when the slow dark hours begin.
May not the darkness hide it from my face?
   You cannot miss that inn.

Shall I meet other wayfarers at night?
   Those who have gone before.
Then must I knock, or call when just in sight?
   They will not keep you standing at that door.

Shall I find comfort, travel-sore and weak?
   Of labour you shall find the sum.
Will there be beds for me and all who seek?
   Yea, beds for all who come.

WILLIAM BLAKE

from Auguries of Innocence

To see a World in a Grain of Sand
And a Heaven in a Wild Flower,
Hold Infinity in the palm of your hand
And Eternity in an hour.

SEAN O'BRIEN

Dignified

Sports Pages: 3. The Olympics

On grim estates at dawn, on college tracks,
In rings, in wheelchairs, velodromes and pools,
While we snore on towards our heart attacks,
They will outstrip the bullet and the fax,
They will rewrite the body and its rules.

Athletes who amazed Zeus and Apollo,
Rivalling their supernatural ease,
Must make do nowadays with us, who follow,
Breathless, on a billion TVs.
Should we believe it's us they aim to please?

The purpose stays essentially the same:
To do what's difficult because they can,
To sign in gold an ordinary name
Across the air from Georgia to Japan,
To change the world by mastering a game.

The rest of us, left waiting at the start,
Still celebrate, as those the gods adore
Today stake everybody's claims for more
By showing life itself becoming art,
Applauded by a planetary roar –

The gun, the clock, the lens, all testify
That those who win take liberties with time:
The sprinter's bow, the vaulter's farewell climb,
The swimmer who escapes her wake, deny
What all the gods insist on, that we die.

ROBERT BROWNING

Pippa's Song

The year's at the spring
And day's at the morn;
Morning's at seven;
The hill-side's dew-pearled;
The lark's on the wing;
The snail's on the thorn:
God's in his heaven –
All's right with the world!

DYLAN THOMAS

And death shall have no dominion

And death shall have no dominion.
Dead men naked they shall be one
With the man in the wind and the west moon;
When their bones are picked clean and the clean bones gone,
They shall have stars at elbow and foot;
Though they go mad they shall be sane,
Though they sink through the sea they shall rise again;
Though lovers be lost love shall not;
And death shall have no dominion.

And death shall have no dominion.
Under the windings of the sea
They lying long shall not die windily;
Twisting on racks when sinews give way,
Strapped to a wheel, yet they shall not break;
Faith in their hands shall snap in two,
And the unicorn evils run them through;
Split all ends up they shan't crack;
And death shall have no dominion.

And death shall have no dominion.
No more may gulls cry at their ears
Or waves break loud on the seashores;
Where blew a flower may a flower no more
Lift its head to the blows of the rain;
Though they be mad and dead as nails,
Heads of the characters hammer through daisies;
Break in the sun till the sun breaks down,
And death shall have no dominion.

JOHN BETJEMAN

Seaside Golf

How straight it flew, how long it flew,
   It clear'd the rutty track
And soaring, disappeared from view
   Beyond the bunker's back –
A glorious, sailing, bounding drive
That made me glad I was alive.

And down the fairway, far along
   It glowed a lonely white;
I played an iron sure and strong
   And clipp'd it out of sight.
And spite of grassy banks between
I knew I'd find it on the green.

And so I did. It lay content
   Two paces from the pin;
A steady putt and then it went
   Oh, most securely in.
The very turf rejoiced to see
That quite unprecedented three.

Ah! seaweed smells from sandy caves
   And thyme and mist in whiffs,
In-coming tide, Atlantic waves
   Slapping the sunny cliffs,
Lark song and sea sounds in the air
And splendour, splendour everywhere.

ARCHILOCHUS

Some Saian sports my splendid shield:
   I had to leave it in a wood,
but saved my skin. Well, I don't care –
   I'll get another just as good.

translated from the Greek by M. L. West

WILLIAM ERNEST HENLEY

Invictus

Out of the night that covers me,
  Black as the Pit from pole to pole,
I thank whatever gods may be
  For my unconquerable soul.

In the fell clutch of circumstance
  I have not winced nor cried aloud.
Under the bludgeonings of chance
  My head is bloody, but unbowed.

Beyond this place of wrath and tears
  Looms but the Horror of the shade,
And yet the menace of the years
  Finds, and shall find, me unafraid.

It matters not how strait the gate,
  How charged with punishments the scroll,
I am the master of my fate:
  I am the captain of my soul.

STEPHEN DUNN

Happiness

A state you must dare not enter
    with hopes of staying,
quicksand in the marshes, and all

the roads leading to a castle
    that doesn't exist.
But there it is, as promised,

with its perfect bridge above
    the crocodiles,
and its doors forever open.

WILLIAM BLAKE

from Milton

And did those feet in ancient time.
Walk upon Englands mountains green:
And was the holy Lamb of God,
On Englands pleasant pastures seen!

And did the Countenance Divine,
Shine forth upon our clouded hills?
And was Jerusalem builded here,
Among these dark Satanic Mills?

Bring me my Bow of burning gold:
Bring me my Arrows of desire:
Bring me my Spear: O clouds unfold!
Bring me my Chariot of fire!

I will not cease from Mental Fight,
Nor shall my Sword sleep in my hand:
Till we have built Jerusalem,
In Englands green & pleasant Land.

ADRIAN MITCHELL

Celia Celia

When I am sad and weary
When I think all hope has gone
When I walk along High Holborn
I think of you with nothing on

THEODORE ROETHKE

The Waking

I wake to sleep, and take my waking slow.
I feel my fate in what I cannot fear.
I learn by going where I have to go.

We think by feeling. What is there to know?
I hear my being dance from ear to ear.
I wake to sleep, and take my waking slow.

Of those so close beside me, which are you?
God bless the Ground! I shall walk softly there,
And learn by going where I have to go.

Light takes the Tree; but who can tell us how?
The lowly worm climbs up a winding stair;
I wake to sleep, and take my waking slow.

Great Nature has another thing to do
To you and me; so take the lively air,
And, lovely, learn by going where to go.

This shaking keeps me steady. I should know.
What falls away is always. And is near.
I wake to sleep, and take my waking slow.
I learn by going where I have to go.

W. B. YEATS

He Wishes for the Cloths of Heaven

Had I the heavens' embroidered cloths,
Enwrought with golden and silver light,
The blue and the dim and the dark cloths
Of night and light and the half-light,
I would spread the cloths under your feet:
But I, being poor, have only my dreams;
I have spread my dreams under your feet;
Tread softly because you tread on my dreams.

ROBERT BLY

Watering the Horse

How strange to think of giving up all ambition!
Suddenly I see with such clear eyes
The white flake of snow
That has just fallen on the horse's mane!

ELIZABETH BARRETT BROWNING

from Sonnets from the Portuguese

XLIII

How do I love thee? Let me count the ways.
I love thee to the depth and breadth and height
My soul can reach, when feeling out of sight
For the ends of Being and ideal Grace.
I love thee to the level of everyday's
Most quiet need, by sun and candlelight.
I love thee freely, as men strive for Right;
I love thee purely, as they turn from Praise.
I love thee with the passion put to use
In my old griefs, and with my childhood's faith.
I love thee with a love I seemed to lose
With my lost saints, – I love thee with the breath,
Smiles, tears, of all my life! – and, if God choose,
I shall but love thee better after death.

WILLIAM WORDSWORTH

My Heart Leaps Up

My heart leaps up when I behold
    A rainbow in the sky:
So was it when my life began;
So is it now I am a man;
So be it when I shall grow old,
    Or let me die!
The Child is father of the Man;
And I could wish my days to be
Bound each to each by natural piety.

DON PATERSON

Being

A version of Rilke

Silent comrade of the distances,
Know that space dilates with your own breath;
ring out, as a bell into the Earth
from the dark rafters of its own high place –

then watch what feeds on you grow strong again.
Learn the transformations through and through:
what in your life has most tormented you?
If the water's sour, turn it into wine.

Our senses cannot fathom this night, so
be the meaning of their strange encounter;
at their crossing, be the radiant centre.

And should the world itself forget your name
say this to the still earth: *I flow.*
Say this to the quick stream: *I am.*

ROBERT FROST

The Road Not Taken

Two roads diverged in a yellow wood,
And sorry I could not travel both
And be one traveller, long I stood
And looked down one as far as I could
To where it bent in the undergrowth;

Then took the other, as just as fair,
And having perhaps the better claim,
Because it was grassy and wanted wear;
Though as for that the passing there
Had worn them really about the same,

And both that morning equally lay
In leaves no step had trodden black.
Oh, I kept the first for another day!
Yet knowing how way leads on to way,
I doubted if I should ever come back.

I shall be telling this with a sigh
Somewhere ages and ages hence:
Two roads diverged in a wood, and I –
I took the one less travelled by,
And that has made all the difference.

EMILY DICKINSON

If I can stop one Heart from breaking
I shall not live in vain
If I can ease one Life the Aching
Or cool one Pain

Or help one fainting Robin
Unto his Nest again
I shall not live in Vain.

EDMUND BLUNDEN

Report on Experience

I have been young, and now am not too old;
And I have seen the righteous forsaken,
His health, his honour and his quality taken.
          This is not what we were formerly told.

I have seen a green country, useful to the race,
Knocked silly with guns and mines, its villages vanished,
Even the last rat and the last kestrel banished –
          God bless us all, this was peculiar grace.

I knew Seraphina; Nature gave her hue,
Glance, sympathy, note, like one from Eden.
I saw her smile warp, heard her lyric deaden;
          She turned to harlotry; – this I took to be new.

Say what you will, our God sees how they run.
These disillusions are His curious proving
That He loves humanity and will go on loving;
          Over there are faith, life, virtue in the sun.

STEVIE SMITH

Conviction

I like to get off with people,
I like to lie in their arms,
I like to be held and tightly kissed,
Safe from all alarms.

I like to laugh and be happy
With a beautiful beautiful kiss,
I tell you, in all the world
There is no bliss like this.

CHRISTINA ROSSETTI

A Christmas Carol

In the bleak mid-winter
  Frosty wind made moan,
Earth stood hard as iron,
  Water like a stone;
Snow had fallen, snow on snow,
  Snow on snow,
In the bleak mid-winter
  Long ago.

Our God, Heaven cannot hold Him
  Nor earth sustain;
Heaven and earth shall flee away
  When He comes to reign:
In the bleak mid-winter
  A stable-place sufficed
The Lord God Almighty
  Jesus Christ.

Enough for Him whom cherubim
  Worship night and day,
A breastful of milk
  And a mangerful of hay;
Enough for Him whom angels
  Fall down before,
The ox and ass and camel
  Which adore.

Angels and archangels
  May have gathered there,
Cherubim and seraphim
  Throng'd the air,
But only His mother
  In her maiden bliss
Worshipped the Beloved
  With a kiss.

What can I give Him,
  Poor as I am?
If I were a shepherd
  I would bring a lamb,
If I were a wise man
  I would do my part, –
Yet what I can I give Him,
  Give my heart.

J. R. R. TOLKIEN

All that is gold does not glitter,
Not all those who wander are lost;
The old that is strong does not wither,
Deep roots are not reached by the frost.

From the ashes a fire shall be woken,
A light from the shadows shall spring;
Renewed shall be blade that was broken,
The crownless again shall be king.

ELIZABETH BISHOP

One Art

The art of losing isn't hard to master;
so many things seem filled with the intent
to be lost that their loss is no disaster.

Lose something every day. Accept the fluster
of lost door keys, the hour badly spent.
The art of losing isn't hard to master.

Then practice losing farther, losing faster:
places, and names, and where it was you meant
to travel. None of these will bring disaster.

I lost my mother's watch. And look! my last, or
next-to-last, of three loved houses went.
The art of losing isn't hard to master.

I lost two cities, lovely ones. And, vaster,
some realms I owned, two rivers, a continent.
I miss them, but it wasn't a disaster.

– Even losing you (the joking voice, a gesture
I love) I shan't have lied. It's evident
the art of losing's not too hard to master
though it may look like (*Write* it!) like disaster.

JOHN MASEFIELD

An Epilogue

I have seen flowers come in stony places
And kind things done by men with ugly faces,
And the gold cup won by the worst horse at the races,
So I trust, too.

THOMAS HARDY

Afterwards

When the Present has latched its postern behind my
     tremulous stay,
  And the May month flaps its glad green leaves like wings,
Delicate-filmed as new-spun silk, will the neighbours say,
  'He was a man who used to notice such things'?

If it be in the dusk when, like an eyelid's soundless blink,
  The dewfall-hawk comes crossing the shades to alight
Upon the wind-warped upland thorn, a gazer may think,
  'To him this must have been a familiar sight.'

If I pass during some nocturnal blackness, mothy and warm,
  When the hedgehog travels furtively over the lawn,
One may say, 'He strove that such innocent creatures should
     come to no harm,
  But he could do little for them; and now he is gone.'

If, when hearing that I have been stilled at last, they stand at
     the door,
  Watching the full-starred heavens that winter sees,
Will this thought rise on those who will meet my face no more,
  'He was one who had an eye for such mysteries'?

And will any say when my bell of quittance is heard in the
     gloom,
  And a crossing breeze cuts a pause in its outrollings,
Till they rise again, as they were a new bell's boom,
  'He hears it not now, but used to notice such things'?

WILLIAM SHAKESPEARE

from Henry V

Act III, Scene i

Once more unto the breach, dear friends, once more,
Or close the wall up with our English dead.
In peace there's nothing so becomes a man
As modest stillness and humility,
But when the blast of war blows in our ears,
Then imitate the action of the tiger.
Stiffen the sinews, conjure up the blood,
Disguise fair nature with hard-favoured rage.
Then lend the eye a terrible aspect,
Let it pry through the portage of the head
Like the brass cannon, let the brow o'erwhelm it
As fearfully as doth a gallèd rock
O'erhang and jutty his confounded base,
Swilled with the wild and wasteful ocean.
Now set the teeth and stretch the nostril wide,
Hold hard the breath, and bend up every spirit
To his full height. On, on, you noblest English,
Whose blood is fet from fathers of war-proof,
Fathers that like so many Alexanders
Have in these parts from morn till even fought,
And sheathed their swords for lack of argument.
Dishonour not your mothers; now attest
That those whom you called fathers did beget you.
Be copy now to men of grosser blood,
And teach them how to war. And you, good yeomen,

Whose limbs were made in England, show us here
The mettle of your pasture; let us swear
That you are worth your breeding – which I doubt not,
For there is none of you so mean and base
That hath not noble lustre in your eyes.
I see you stand like greyhounds in the slips,
Straining upon the start. The game's afoot.
Follow your spirit, and upon this charge
Cry, 'God for Harry! England and Saint George!'

Thinking of England

And let the lesson to be – to be yersel's,
Ye needna fash gin it's to be ocht else.
To be yersel's – and to mak' that worth bein' . . .

Hugh MacDiarmid
'A Drunk Man Looks at a Thistle'

Let me take you on a journey to a foreign land . . .
William Hague

I

Dusk-light; the news tells of another train derailed,
and shoppers buying up the shops, and livestock
being herded to the chop – their chops unfit to eat –
and politicians once more putting foot to mouth.
Through my east-end window –

over the tangled tree,
the council houses: some sardined with children,
catering-sized gallon tubs of cooking oil empty beside their
    bins;
some sheltering one of the three million children still in
    poverty;
some sold to Thatcher's fortunate –
now worth hundreds of thousands, more,
with rents devised to make even the well-off poor –
over the kids and dogs on a hanky of grass,
the burnt-out car, the hush-hush trendy warehouse bar,
ISLAM UNITE scrawled on a wall –

a man's voice trails its skittering wail across the sky,
and all around me people are preparing to pray
to a God to whom I am one of the damned.

II

And what did our great-grandmothers taste?
Perhaps pie and mash and jellied eels, or hash, pease
    pudding,
cobbler, cottage pie,
                        pasties and pickled eggs.
When I was small there was still Spam and jellied ham –
semolina, parkin, treacle tart.
Why have we not stood with our mothers,
floured and flushed beside the oven door,
watching our first Yorkshire puddings:
how their globed bellies swell?
Why was this not passed daughter to daughter?
When did the passing stop?
When did we choose to steal instead
from the daughters of all those we have hated or hurt:
gnocchi, noodles, couscous, naan, falafel, jerk?
For dinner I have chicken dupiaza from a foil tray –
how fitting England's national dish is not homemade but
    takeaway.
Through thrift – the rent is due – I boil my own rice up,
long-grain American.

III

You're so fortunate, they would exclaim, as I took photographs
of them beside King's Chapel, or of willows washing
their hair in the Cam, *to have all of this history around you.*

England's history is medieval pogroms;
it is Elizabeth, her skin a crust of Dover-white,
loosing galleons to pillage fruits, tobacco, men.
The bulging-eyed thieves swinging to the crowd's delight
metres from Shakespeare's Globe;

                                     stripping the churches;
Becket bleeding buckets on the floor;
and work-houses for the poor,
and the slave-trade; and raping the wife –
lie back and think of ... crinolines, Crimea.
Missionaries hacking their one true path through the jungle.
Winston swearing: *We will fight them on the beaches!*

These people held the cargo of my genes within their blood.
Not all were good.

                     But how can I be held up as
                     accountable?
And yet, all of the good they earned, and blessed me with
brings with it blame. Today I filled a form in –
ticked *White British* with a cringe of shame.

I am educated, middle-class, housed, well.
I am fat and rich on history's hell.

IV

I remember bracken, and heather, and a gusty, gutsy
wind, and a plastic tub of windberries that filled
and emptied, its ink writing a whodunit on my face.

I remember Southport, where granny said fine ladies had once
gone to purchase linens, and the best. Catching the miniature
train down to Happy-Land, and my name in wet sand,

and my grandfather towelling the sand off my legs,
and then our picnic in the car – tinned salmon sandwiches,
a flask of tea, crosswords. A Penguin biscuit.

I remember sitting in an American bar having to squint
to read about abortion laws by the dim candlelight,
and sipping my six-dollar Cosmopolitan – with a dollar tip –

and thinking of our local; its open fire, the rain
on its windows, and you in it. Maybe on a Sunday
after a walk on the heath, and lamb with mint sauce,
and thinking how I never could leave.

v

Just finishing off the curry, when the football starts.
An England game. Satellites are readying themselves
to bounce the match around the globe,
and prove that we are not the power we were.

The crowd belts out 'God Save the Queen',
though they do not believe in God or Queen;
their strips red, white and blue –
two of these being borrowed hues; loaned colours we use
to drown out the white noise of ourselves.
We are the whitest of the white:

                                        once this meant *right* –
Christ's holy light; the opposite of night, or black –
but now it only points to lack, the blank of who we are.

Who ever celebrates St George's Day?
And did you hear the one about the Englishman ...?

A friend of mine at home's a Bolton Wanderers fan:
they chant *White Army.*

VI

And then the news again, at ten –
sometimes it makes you want to pack and leave it all:

the floods, the fuel, the teacher shortage in the schools,
the bombing of Iraq, the heart attacks, long working hours
and little sex, racist police, cigarette tax, grants all axed,
three million children still in poverty,
the burnt out car, the takeaway,
the headlines about Krauts, the lager louts,
the wobbly bridge they built, the colonial guilt,
the needless pain, the rain, the rain,
the pogroms, the pink globe, the tangled tree,
the Raj, the rape, the linens,
all the endless fucking cups of tea . . .

but everyone speaks English now,

and sometimes, a voice trails its skittering wail across the sky,
and I feel not just gratitude, but pride.

ELLA WHEELER WILCOX

Solitude

Laugh, and the world laughs with you;
    Weep, and you weep alone;
For the sad old earth must borrow its mirth,
    But has trouble enough of its own.
Sing, and the hills will answer;
    Sigh, it is lost on the air;
The echoes bound to a joyful sound,
    But shrink from voicing care.

Rejoice, and men will seek you;
    Grieve, and they turn and go;
They want full measure of all your pleasure,
    But they do not need your woe.
Be glad, and your friends are many;
    Be sad, and you lose them all, –
There are none to decline your nectared wine,
    But alone you must drink life's gall.

Feast, and your halls are crowded;
    Fast, and the world goes by.
Succeed and give, and it helps you live,
    But no man can help you die.
There is room in the halls of pleasure
    For a large and lordly train,
But one by one we must all file on
    Through the narrow aisles of pain.

DOROTHY PARKER

Penelope

In the pathway of the sun,
  In the footsteps of the breeze,
Where the world and sky are one,
  He shall ride the silver seas,
    He shall cut the glittering wave.
I shall sit at home, and rock;
Rise, to heed a neighbour's knock;
Brew my tea, and snip my thread;
Bleach the linen for my bed.
    They will call him brave.

ALICE OSWALD

Wedding

From time to time our love is like a sail
and when the sail begins to alternate
from tack to tack, it's like a swallowtail
and when the swallow flies it's like a coat;
and if the coat is yours, it has a tear
like a wide mouth and when the mouth begins
to draw the wind, it's like a trumpeter
and when the trumpet blows, it blows like millions . . .
and this, my love, when millions come and go
beyond the need of us, is like a trick;
and when the trick begins, it's like a toe
tip-toeing on a rope, which is like luck;
and when the luck begins, it's like a wedding,
which is like love, which is like everything.

Warning to Children

Children, if you dare to think
Of the greatness, rareness, muchness,
Fewness of this precious only
Endless world in which you say
You live, you think of things like this:
Blocks of slate enclosing dappled
Red and green, enclosing tawny
Yellow nets, enclosing white
And black acres of dominoes,
Where a neat brown paper parcel
Tempts you to untie the string.
In the parcel a small island,
On the island a large tree,
On the tree a husky fruit.
Strip the husk and pare the rind off:
In the kernel you will see
Blocks of slate enclosed by dappled
Red and green, enclosed by tawny
Yellow nets, enclosed by white
And black acres of dominoes,
Where the same brown paper parcel –
Children, leave the string alone!
For who dares undo the parcel
Finds himself at once inside it,
On the island, in the fruit,
Blocks of slate about his head,
Finds himself enclosed by dappled

Green and red, enclosed by yellow
Tawny nets, enclosed by black
And white acres of dominoes,
With the same brown paper parcel
Still unopened on his knee.
And, if he then should dare to think
Of the fewness, muchness, rareness,
Greatness of this endless only
Precious world in which he says
He lives – he then unties the string.

GEORGE HERBERT

Prayer

Prayer the Churches banquet, Angels age,
   Gods breath in man returning to his birth,
   The soul in paraphrase, heart in pilgrimage,
The Christian plummet sounding heav'n and earth;

Engine against th' Almightie, sinners towre,
   Reversed thunder, Christ-side-piercing spear,
   The six-daies – world transposing in an houre,
A kinde of tune, which all things heare and fear;

Softnesse, and peace, and joy, and love, and blisse,
   Exalted Manna, gladnesse of the best,
   Heaven in ordinarie, man well drest,
The milkie may, the bird of Paradise,
   Church-bels beyond the starres heard, the souls bloud,
   The land of spices; something understood.

SEAMUS HEANEY

from Markings

I

We marked the pitch: four jackets for four goalposts,
That was all. The corners and the squares
Were there like longitude and latitude
Under the bumpy ground, to be
Agreed about or disagreed about
When the time came. And then we picked the teams
And crossed the line our called names drew between us.

Youngsters shouting their heads off in a field
As the light died and they kept on playing
Because by then they were playing in their heads
And the actual kicked ball came to them
Like a dream heaviness, and their own hard
Breathing in the dark and skids on grass
Sounded like effort in another world . . .
It was quick and constant, a game that never need
Be played out. Some limit had been passed,
There was fleetness, furtherance, untiredness
In time that was extra, unforeseen and free.

A. E. HOUSMAN

from A Shropshire Lad

II

Loveliest of trees, the cherry now
Is hung with bloom along the bough,
And stands about the woodland ride
Wearing white for Eastertide.

Now, of my threescore years and ten,
Twenty will not come again,
And take from seventy springs a score,
It only leaves me fifty more.

And since to look at things in bloom
Fifty springs are little room,
About the woodlands I will go
To see the cherry hung with snow.

WENDY COPE

Two Cures for Love

1. Don't see him. Don't phone or write a letter.
2. The easy way: get to know him better.

JOHN DRYDEN

Happy the Man

Horace, Odes, Book III, xxix

Happy the man, and happy he alone,
   He who can call today his own:
   He who, secure within, can say,
Tomorrow do thy worst, for I have lived today.
   Be fair or foul or rain or shine
The joys I have possessed, in spite of fate, are mine.
Not Heaven itself upon the past has power,
But what has been, has been, and I have had my hour.

SIEGFRIED SASSOON

Everyone Sang

Everyone suddenly burst out singing;
And I was filled with such delight
As prisoned birds must find in freedom,
Winging wildly across the white
Orchards and dark-green fields; on – on – and out of sight.

Everyone's voice was suddenly lifted;
And beauty came like the setting sun:
My heart was shaken with tears; and horror
Drifted away . . . O, but Everyone
Was a bird; and the song was wordless; the singing will never
    be done.

SHMUEL HANAGID

Soar, Don't Settle

Soar, don't settle for earth
    and sky – soar to Orion;
and be strong, but not like an ox or mule
    that's driven – strong like a lion.

translated from the Hebrew by Peter Cole

LANGSTON HUGHES

I, Too

I, too, sing America.

I am the darker brother.
They send me to eat in the kitchen
When company comes,
But I laugh,
And eat well,
And grow strong.

Tomorrow,
I'll be at the table
When company comes.
Nobody'll dare
Say to me,
'Eat in the kitchen,'
Then.

Besides,
They'll see how beautiful I am
And be ashamed –

I, too, am America.

JOHN KEATS

On First Looking into Chapman's Homer

Much have I travell'd in the realms of gold,
   And many goodly states and kingdoms seen;
   Round many western islands have I been
Which bards in fealty to Apollo hold.
Oft of one wide expanse had I been told
   That deep-brow'd Homer ruled as his demesne;
   Yet did I never breathe its pure serene
Till I heard Chapman speak out loud and bold:
Then felt I like some watcher of the skies
   When a new planet swims into his ken;
Or like stout Cortez when with eagle eyes
   He star'd at the Pacific – and all his men
Look'd at each other with a wild surmise –
   Silent, upon a peak in Darien.

ROBERT HERRICK

The End

Conquer we shall, but we must first contend;
'Tis not the Fight that crowns us, but the end.

Climbing

High up in the apple tree climbing I go,
With the sky above me, the earth below.
Each branch is the step of a wonderful
    stair
Which leads to the town I see shining up
    there.

Climbing, climbing, higher and higher,
The branches blow and I see a spire,
The gleam of a turret, the glint of a dome,
All sparkling and bright, like white sea
    foam.

On and on, from bough to bough,
The leaves are thick, but I push my way
    through;
Before, I have always had to stop,
But today I am sure I shall reach the top.

Today to the end of the marvelous stair,
Where those glittering pinnacles flash in
    the air!
Climbing, climbing, higher I go,
With the sky close above me, the earth
    far below.

WILLIAM SHAKESPEARE

from Richard II

Act II, Scene i

This royal throne of kings, this sceptred isle,
This earth of majesty, this seat of Mars,
This other Eden, demi-paradise,
This fortress built by nature for herself
Against infection and the hand of war,
This happy breed of men, this little world,
This precious stone set in the silver sea,
Which serves it in the office of a wall,
Or as a moat defensive to a house
Against the envy of less happier lands;
This blessèd plot, this earth, this realm, this England . . .

MARIANNE MOORE

I May, I Might, I Must

If you will tell me why the fen
appears impassable, I then
will tell you why I think that I
can get across it if I try.

MAURA DOOLEY

Freight

I am the ship in which you sail,
little dancing bones,
your passage between the dream
and the waking dream,
your sieve, your pea-green boat.
I'll pay whatever toll your ferry needs.
And you, whose history's already charted
in a rope of cells, be tender to
those other unnamed vessels
who will surprise you one day,
tug-tugging, irresistible,
and float you out beyond your depth,
where you'll look down, puzzled, amazed.

If –

er Square-Toes' – Rewards and Fairies

If you can keep your head when all about you
    Are losing theirs and blaming it on you,
If you can trust yourself when all men doubt you,
    But make allowance for their doubting too;
If you can wait and not be tired by waiting,
    Or being lied about, don't deal in lies,
Or being hated, don't give way to hating,
    And yet don't look too good, nor talk too wise:

If you can dream – and not make dreams your master;
    If you can think – and not make thoughts your aim;
If you can meet with Triumph and Disaster
    And treat those two impostors just the same;
If you can bear to hear the truth you've spoken
    Twisted by knaves to make a trap for fools,
Or watch the things you gave your life to, broken,
    And stoop and build 'em up with worn-out tools:

If you can make one heap of all your winnings
    And risk it on one turn of pitch-and-toss,
And lose, and start again at your beginnings
    And never breathe a word about your loss;
If you can force your heart and nerve and sinew
    To serve your turn long after they are gone,
And so hold on when there is nothing in you
    Except the Will which says to them: 'Hold on!'

If you can talk with crowds and keep your virtue,
    Or walk with Kings – nor lose the common touch,
If neither foes nor loving friends can hurt you,
    If all men count with you, but none too much;
If you can fill the unforgiving minute
    With sixty seconds' worth of distance run,
Yours is the Earth and everything that's in it,
    And – which is more – you'll be a Man, my son!

PASTOR NIEMÖLLER

First they came for the Jews
and I did not speak out –
because I was not a Jew.
Then they came for the communists
and I did not speak out –
because I was not a communist.
Then they came for the trade unionists
and I did not speak out –
because I was not a trade unionist.
Then they came for me –
and there was no one left
to speak out for me.

CHARLES CAUSLEY

I Am the Song

I am the song that sings the bird.
I am the leaf that grows the land.
I am the tide that moves the moon.
I am the stream that halts the sand.
I am the cloud that drives the storm.
I am the earth that lights the sun.
I am the fire that strikes the stone.
I am the clay that shapes the hand.
I am the word that speaks the man.

KATHLEEN JAMIE

The Way We Live

Pass the tambourine, let me bash out praises
to the Lord God of movement, to Absolute
non-friction, flight, and the scarey side:
death by avalanche, birth by failed contraception.
Of chicken tandoori and reggae, loud, from tenements,
commitment, driving fast and unswerving
friendship. Of tee-shirts on pulleys, giros and Bombay,
barmen, dreaming waitresses with many fake-gold
bangles. Or airports, impulse, and waking to uncertainty,
to strip-lights, motorways, or that pantheon –
the mountains. To overdrafts and grafting

and the fit slow pulse of wipers as you're
creeping over Rannoch, while the God of moorland
walks abroad with his entourage of freezing fog,
his bodyguard of snow.
Of endless gloaming in the North, of Asiatic swelter,
to launderettes, anecdotes, passions and exhaustion,
Final Demands and dead men, the skeletal grip
of government. To misery and elation; mixed,
the sod and caprice of landlords.
To the way it fits, the way it is, the way it seems
to be: let me bash out praises – pass the tambourine.

ROBERT FROST

Riders

The surest thing there is is we are riders,
And though none too successful at it, guiders,
Through everything presented, land and tide
And now the very air, of what we ride.

What is this talked-of mystery of birth
But being mounted bareback on the earth?
We can just see the infant up astride,
His small fist buried in the bushy hide.

There is our wildest mount – a headless horse.
But though it runs unbridled off its course,
And all our blandishments would seem defied,
We have ideas yet that we haven't tried.

COLETTE BRYCE

Early Version

Our boat was slow to reach Bethsaida; winds oppressed us,
fast and cold, our hands were blistered from the oars.
We'd done to death our songs and jokes, with miles
to go, when Jesus spoke:

he said he'd crouched upon the shore, alone, engaged
in silent prayer, when, looking down, he started –
saw his own image crouching there. And when he leant
and dipped his hand

he swore he felt the fingers touch, and as he rose
the image stood and, slowly, each put out a foot
and took a step, and where they met, the weight of one
annulled the other;

then how he'd moved across the lake, walked on the soles
of his liquid self, and he described how cool it felt
on his aching, dusty feet; the way he'd strode a steady
course to board the boat

where we now sat – mesmerized. He gestured out
towards the shore, along the lake, then to himself,
and asked us all to visualize, to open what he always
called our 'fettered minds'.

ALFRED, LORD TENNYSON

The Charge of the Light Brigade

I

Half a league, half a league,
  Half a league onward,
All in the valley of Death
  Rode the six hundred.
'Forward, the Light Brigade!
Charge for the guns!' he said:
Into the valley of Death
  Rode the six hundred.

II

'Forward, the Light Brigade!'
Was there a man dismayed?
Not though the soldier knew
  Some one had blundered:
Their's not to make reply,
Their's not to reason why,
Their's but to do and die:
Into the valley of Death
  Rode the six hundred.

III

Cannon to right of them,
Cannon to left of them,
Cannon in front of them
  Volleyed and thundered;

Stormed at with shot and shell,
Boldly they rode and well,
Into the jaws of Death,
Into the mouth of Hell
   Rode the six hundred.

IV

Flashed all their sabres bare,
Flashed as they turned in air
Sabring the gunners there,
Charging an army, while
   All the world wondered:
Plunged in the battery-smoke
Right through the line they broke;
Cossack and Russian
Reeled from the sabre-stroke
   Shattered and sundered.
Then they rode back, but not
   Not the six hundred.

V

Cannon to right of them,
Cannon to left of them,
Cannon behind them
   Volleyed and thundered;
Stormed at with shot and shell,
While horse and hero fell,
They that had fought so well
Came through the jaws of Death,
Back from the mouth of Hell,
All that was left of them,
   Left of six hundred.

When can their glory fade?
O the wild charge they made!
 All the world wondered.
Honour the charge they made!
Honour the Light Brigade,
 Noble six hundred!

SIMON ARMITAGE

Let me put it this way:
if you came to lay

your sleeping head
against my arm or sleeve,

and if my arm went dead,
or if I had to take my leave

at midnight, I should rather
cleave it from the joint or seam

than make a scene
or bring you round.

There,
how does that sound?

W. B. YEATS

An Irish Airman Foresees His Death

I know that I shall meet my fate
Somewhere among the clouds above;
Those that I fight I do not hate,
Those that I guard I do not love;
My country is Kiltartan Cross,
My countrymen Kiltartan's poor,
No likely end could bring them loss
Or leave them happier than before.
Nor law, nor duty bade me fight,
Nor public men, nor cheering crowds;
A lonely impulse of delight
Drove to this tumult in the clouds;
I balanced all, brought all to mind,
The years to come seemed waste of breath,
A waste of breath the years behind
In balance with this life, this death.

SHEENAGH PUGH

Envying Owen Beattie

To have stood on the Arctic island
by the graves where Franklin's men
buried their shipmates: good enough.

To hack through the permafrost
to the coffin, its loving plaque
cut from a tin can: better.

And freeing the lid, seeing
the young sailor cocooned in ice,
asleep in his glass case.

Then melting it so gently, inch
by inch, a hundred years
and more falling away, all the distance

of death a soft hiss of steam
on the air, till at last they cupped
two feet, bare and perfect,

in their hands, and choked up,
because it was any feet
poking out of the bedclothes.

And when the calm, pinched
twenty-year-old face
came free, and he lay there,

five foot four of authentic
Victorian adventurer, tuberculous,
malnourished, John Torrington

the stoker, who came so far
in the cold, and someone whispered,
It's like he's unconscious.

Then Beattie stooped, lifted him
out of bed, the six stone
limp in his arms, and the head lolled

and rested on his shoulder,
and he felt the rush
that reckless trust sends

through parents and lovers. To have him
like that, the frail, diseased
little time-traveller,

to feel the lashes prickle
your cheek, to be that close
to the parted lips.

You would know all the fairy-tales
spoke true; how could you not try
to wake him with a kiss?

WALTER DE LA MARE

Fare Well

When I lie where shades of darkness
Shall no more assail mine eyes,
Nor the rain make lamentation
    When the wind sighs;
How will fare the world whose wonder
Was the very proof of me?
Memory fades, must the remembered
    Perishing be?

Oh, when this my dust surrenders
Hand, foot, lip, to dust again,
May these loved and loving faces
    Please other men!
May the rusting harvest hedgerow
Still the Traveller's Joy entwine,
And as happy children gather
    Posies once mine.

Look thy last on all things lovely,
Every hour. Let no night
Seal thy sense in deathly slumber
    Till to delight
Thou have paid thy utmost blessing;
Since that all things thou wouldst praise
Beauty took from those who loved them
    In other days.

We two boys together clinging,
One the other never leaving,
Up and down the roads going, North and South
    excursions making,
Power enjoying, elbows stretching, fingers clutching,
Arm'd and fearless, eating, drinking, sleeping, loving,
No law less than ourselves owning, sailing, soldiering,
    thieving, threatening,
Misers, menials, priests alarming, air breathing, water
    drinking, on the turf or the sea-beach dancing,
Cities wrenching, ease scorning, statutes mocking,
    feebleness chasing,
Fulfilling our foray.

LEONARDO DA VINCI

He turns not back who is bound to a star.
Obstacles do not bend me.
Every obstacle yields to stern resolve.

translated from the Latin by Jean Paul Richter

JALALUDDIN RUMI

Come, come, for you will not find another friend like Me,
Where indeed is a Beloved like Me in all the world?
Come, come, and do not spend your life in wandering,
Since there is no market elsewhere for your money.
You are as a dry valley, and I as the rain,
You are as a ruined city, and I as the Architect.
Except My service, which is Joy's sunrise,
Man never has felt and never will feel an impression of Joy.

translated from the Persian by Professor R. A. Nicholson

ROGER MCGOUGH

The Way Things Are

No, the candle is not crying, it cannot feel pain.
Even telescopes, like the rest of us, grow bored.
Bubblegum will not make the hair soft and shiny.
The duller the imagination, the faster the car –
I am your father and this is the way things are

When the sky is looking the other way,
do not enter the forest. No, the wind
is not caused by the rushing of clouds.
An excuse is as good a reason as any.
A lighthouse, launched, will not go far –
I am your father and this is the way things are

No, old people do not walk slowly
because they have plenty of time.
Gardening books when buried will not flower.
Though lightly worn, a crown may leave a scar –
I am your father and this is the way things are

No, the red woolly hat has not been
put on the railing to keep it warm.
When one glove is missing, both are lost.
Today's craft fair is tomorrow's car boot sale.
The guitarist gently weeps, not the guitar –
I am your father and this is the way things are

Pebbles work best without batteries.
The deckchair will fail as a unit of currency.
Even though your shadow is shortening
it does not mean you are growing smaller.
Moonbeams sadly, will not survive in a jar –
I am your father and this is the way things are

For centuries the bullet remained quietly confident
that the gun would be invented.
A drowning Dadaist will not appreciate
the concrete lifebelt.
No guarantee my last goodbye is au revoir –
I am your father and this is the way things are

Do not become a prison-officer unless you know
what you're letting someone else in for.
The thrill of being a shower curtain will soon pall.
No trusting hand awaits the falling star –
I am your father, and I am sorry,
but this is the way things are.

MARY E. FRYE

Do not stand at my grave and weep;
I am not there. I do not sleep.
I am a thousand winds that blow.
I am the diamond glints on snow.
I am the sunlight on ripened grain.
I am the gentle autumn rain.
When you awaken in the morning's hush
I am the swift uplifting rush
Of quiet birds in circled flight.
I am the soft stars that shine at night.
Do not stand at my grave and cry;
I am not there. I did not die.

MAYA ANGELOU

I Know Why the Caged Bird Sings

The free bird leaps
on the back of the win
and floats downstream
till the current ends
and dips his wings
in the orange sun rays
and dares to claim the sky.

But a bird that stalks
down his narrow cage
can seldom see through
his bars of rage
his wings are clipped and
his feet are tied
so he opens his throat to sing.

The caged bird sings
with fearful trill
of the things unknown
but longed for still
and is tune is heard
on the distant hill for the caged bird
sings of freedom

The free bird thinks of another breeze
an the trade winds soft through the sighing trees
and the fat worms waiting on a dawn-bright lawn
and he names the sky his own.

But a caged bird stands on the grave of dreams
his shadow shouts on a nightmare scream
his wings are clipped and his feet are tied
so he opens his throat to sing

The caged bird sings
with a fearful trill
of things unknown
but longed for still
and his tune is heard
on the distant hill
for the caged bird
sings of freedom.

MATTHEW ARNOLD

Dover Beach

The sea is calm to-night.
The tide is full, the moon lies fair
Upon the straits; – on the French coast the light
Gleams and is gone; the cliffs of England stand,
Glimmering and vast, out in the tranquil bay.
Come to the window, sweet is the night-air!
Only, from the long line of spray
Where the sea meets the moon-blanch'd land,
Listen! you hear the grating roar
Of pebbles which the waves draw back, and fling,
At their return, up the high strand,
Begin, and cease, and then again begin,
With tremulous cadence slow, and bring
The eternal note of sadness in.

Sophocles long ago
Heard it on the Aegean, and it brought
Into his mind the turbid ebb and flow
Of human misery; we
Find also in the sound a thought,
Hearing it by this distant northern sea.

The Sea of Faith
Was once, too, at the full, and round earth's shore
Lay like the folds of a bright girdle furl'd.
But now I only hear
Its melancholy, long, withdrawing roar,
Retreating, to the breath
Of the night-wind, down the vast edges drear
And naked shingles of the world.

Ah, love, let us be true
To one another! for the world, which seems
To lie before us like a land of dreams,
So various, so beautiful, so new,
Hath really neither joy, nor love, nor light,
Nor certitude, nor peace, nor help for pain;
And we are here as on a darkling plain
Swept with confused alarms of struggle and flight.
Where ignorant armies clash by night.

U. A. FANTHORPE

Atlas

There is a kind of love called maintenance,
Which stores the WD40 and knows when to use it;

Which checks the insurance, and doesn't forget
The milkman; which remembers to plant bulbs;

Which answers letters; which knows the way
The money goes; which deals with dentists

And Road Fund Tax and meeting trains,
And postcards to the lonely; which upholds

The permanently ricketty elaborate
Structures of living, which is Atlas.

And maintenance is the sensible side of love,
Which knows what time and weather are doing
To my brickwork; insulates my faulty wiring;
Laughs at my dryrotten jokes; remembers
My need for gloss and grouting; which keeps
My suspect edifice upright in air,
As Atlas did the sky.

ANON

Life's Variety

Why do we grumble because a tree is bent,
When, in our streets, there are even men who are bent?
Why must we complain that the new moon is slanting?
Can anyone reach the skies to straighten it?
Can't we see that some cocks have combs on their heads,
    but no plumes in their tails?
And some have plumes in their tails, but no claws on their
    toes?
And others have claws on their toes, but no power to crow?
He who has a head has no cap to wear, and he who has a
    cap has no head to wear it on.
The Owa has everything but a horse's stable.
Some great scholars of Ifa cannot tell the way to Ofa.
Others know the way to Ofa, but not one line of Ifa.
Great eaters have no food to eat, and great drinkers no wine
    to drink:
Wealth has a coat of many colours.

translated from the Yoruba by Chinweizu

WILLIAM BLAKE

The Angel that presided o'er my birth
Said, 'Little creature, form'd of Joy and Mirth,
'Go love without the help of any Thing on Earth.'

W. H. AUDEN

As I walked out one evening,
  Walking down Bristol Street,
The crowds upon the pavement
  Were fields of harvest wheat.

And down by the brimming river
  I heard a lover sing
Under an arch of the railway:
  'Love has no ending.

'I'll love you, dear, I'll love you
  Till China and Africa meet,
And the river jumps over the mountain
  And the salmon sing in the street,

'I'll love you till the ocean
  Is folded and hung up to dry
And the seven stars go squawking
  Like geese about the sky.

'The years shall run like rabbits,
  For in my arms I hold
The Flower of the Ages,
  And the first love of the world.'

But all the clocks in the city
  Began to whirr and chime:
'O let not Time deceive you,
  You cannot conquer Time.

'In the burrows of the Nightmare
    Where Justice naked is,
Time watches from the shadow
    And coughs when you would kiss.

'In headaches and in worry
    Vaguely life leaks away,
And Time will have his fancy
    Tomorrow or today.

'Into many a green valley
    Drifts the appalling snow;
Time breaks the threaded dances
    And the diver's brilliant bow.

'O plunge your hands in water,
    Plunge them in up to the wrist;
Stare, stare in the basin
    And wonder what you've missed.

'The glacier knocks in the cupboard,
    The desert sighs in the bed,
And the crack in the tea-cup opens
    A lane to the land of the dead.

'Where the beggars raffle the banknotes
    And the Giant is enchanting to Jack,
And the Lily-white Boy is a Roarer,
    And Jill goes down on her back.

'O look, look in the mirror,
    O look in your distress;
Life remains a blessing
    Although you cannot bless.

'O stand, stand at the window
    As the tears scald and start;
You shall love your crooked neighbour
    With your crooked heart.'

It was late, late in the evening,
    The lovers they were gone;
The clocks had ceased their chiming
    And the deep river ran on.

JOHN CLARE

'I Am'

I am – yet what I am, none cares or knows;
　My friends forsake me like a memory lost: –
I am the self-consumer of my woes; –
　They rise and vanish in oblivion's host,
Like shadows in love's frenzied stifled throes: –
And yet I am, and live – like vapours tost

Into the nothingness of scorn and noise, –
　Into the living sea of waking dreams,
Where there is neither sense of life or joys,
　But the vast shipwreck of my life's esteems;
Even the dearest, that I love the best
Are strange – nay, rather stranger than the rest.

I long for scenes, where man hath never trod
　A place where woman never smiled or wept
There to abide with my Creator, God;
　And sleep as I in childhood, sweetly slept,
Untroubling, and untroubled where I lie,
The grass below – above, the vaulted sky.

WILLIAM WORDSWORTH

The Daffodils

I wander'd lonely as a cloud
That floats on high o'er vales and hills,
When all at once I saw a crowd,
A host of golden daffodils,
Beside the lake, beneath the trees
Fluttering and dancing in the breeze.

Continuous as the stars that shine
And twinkle on the milky way,
They stretch'd in never-ending line
Along the margin of a bay:
Ten thousand saw I at a glance
Tossing their heads in sprightly dance.

The waves beside them danced, but they
Out-did the sparkling waves in glee: —
A Poet could not but be gay
In such a jocund company!
I gazed – and gazed – but little thought
What wealth the show to me had brought.

For oft, when on my couch I lie
In vacant or in pensive mood,
They flash upon that inward eye
Which is the bliss of solitude;
And then my heart with pleasure fills
And dances with the daffodils.

ANNE BRADSTREET

To my Dear and Loving Husband

If ever two were one, then surely we.
If ever man were loved by wife, then thee;
If ever wife was happy in a man,
Compare with me, ye women, if you can.
I prize thy love more than whole mines of gold
Or all the riches that the East doth hold.
My love is such that rivers cannot quench,
Nor ought but love from thee, give recompense.
Thy love is such I can no way repay,
The heavens reward thee manifold, I pray.
Then while we live, in love let's so persevere
That when we live no more, we may live ever.

PABLO NERUDA

Dead Woman

If suddenly you do not exist,
if suddenly you no longer live,
I shall live on.

I do not dare,
I do not dare to write it,
if you die.

I shall live on.

For where a man has no voice,
there shall be my voice.

Where blacks are flogged and beaten,
I cannot be dead.
When my brothers go to prison
I shall go with them.

When victory,
not my victory,
but the great victory
comes,
even if I am dumb I must speak;
I shall see it coming even if I am blind.

No, forgive me.
If you no longer live,

if you, beloved, my love,
if you
have died,
all the leaves will fall on my breast,
it will rain on my soul night and day,
the snow will burn my heart,
I shall walk with frost and fire and death and snow,
my feet will want to walk to where you are sleeping,
but
I shall stay alive,
because above all things you wanted me
indomitable,
and, my love, because you know that I am not only a man
but all mankind.

translated from the Spanish by Brian Cole

JACKIE KAY

Holy Island

All winter I was waiting
for something to give
and today I felt it,
a small crack,
the sun on the sandy dunes
by the Causeway,
the feeling of the land
so close to the sea.
Nick and me and the dog
striding along
by the old Benedictine monastery
till we walked into
a new vocabulary –
hope, benevolence, benediction –
after the long wintering
of false starts,
the same day over and over,
the spring at last here –
I said a small prayer,
the wind on my hair.

ANDREW MARVELL

from Thoughts in a Garden

What wondrous life is this I lead!
Ripe apples drop about my head;
The luscious clusters of the vine
Upon my mouth do crush their wine;
The nectarine and curious peach
Into my hands themselves do reach;
Stumbling on melons, as I pass,
Ensnared with flowers, I fall on grass.

Meanwhile the mind from pleasure less
Withdraws into its happiness:
The mind, that Ocean where each kind
Does straight its own resemblance find;
Yet it creates, transcending these,
Far other worlds, and other seas;
Annihilating all that's made
To a green thought in a green shade.

PHILIP LARKIN

The Trees

The trees are coming into leaf
Like something almost being said;
The recent buds relax and spread,
Their greenness is a kind of grief.

Is it that they are born again
And we grow old? No, they die too.
Their yearly trick of looking new
Is written down in rings of grain.

Yet still the unresting castles thresh
In fullgrown thickness every May.
Last year is dead, they seem to say,
Begin afresh, afresh, afresh.

DEREK MAHON

Everything is Going to Be All Right

How should I not be glad to contemplate
the clouds clearing beyond the dormer window
and a high tide reflected on the ceiling?
There will be dying, there will be dying,
but there is no need to go into that.
The poems flow from the hand unbidden
and the hidden source is the watchful heart.
The sun rises in spite of everything
and the far cities are beautiful and bright.
I lie here in a riot of sunlight
watching the day break and the clouds flying.
Everything is going to be all right.

from Prometheus Unbound

To suffer woes which Hope thinks infinite;
To forgive wrongs darker than death or nights;
To defy Power, which seems omnipotent;
To love, and bear; to Hope till Hope creates
From its own wreck the thing it contemplates;
Neither to change, nor falter, nor repent;
This, like thy glory, Titan is to be
Good, great and joyous, beautiful and free;
This is alone Life, Joy, Empire, and Victory.

EDWARD THOMAS

Adlestrop

Yes. I remember Adlestrop –
The name, because one afternoon
Of heat the express-train drew up there
Unwontedly. It was late June.

The steam hissed. Some one cleared his throat.
No one left and no one came
On the bare platform. What I saw
Was Adlestrop – only the name

And willows, willow-herb, and grass,
And meadowsweet, and haycocks dry,
No whit less still and lonely fair
Than the high cloudlets in the sky.

And for that minute a blackbird sang
Close by, and around him, mistier,
Farther and farther, all the birds
Of Oxfordshire and Gloucestershire.

SIR HENRY WOTTON

The Character of a Happy Life

How happy is he born and taught,
That serveth not another's will;
Whose Armour is his honest thought,
And simple truth his utmost skill;

Whose passions not his Masters are;
Whose Soul is still prepar'd for Death,
Unti'd unto the World by care
Of public Fame, or private Breath;

Who envies none that chance doth raise,
Or vice; who never understood
How deepest Wounds are given by praise;
Nor Rules of State, but Rules of good;

Who hath his Life from Rumours freed;
Whose Conscience is his strong retreat;
Whose State can neither Flatterers feed,
Nor Ruin make Oppressors great;

Who God doth late and early pray
More of his Grace than Gifts to lend;
And entertains the harmless day
With a Religious book or friend!

This man is freed from servile bands
Of hope to rise, or fear to fall:
Lord of himself, though not of lands;
And having nothing, yet hath all.

i thank You God for most this amazing
day:for the leaping greenly spirits of trees
and a blue true dream of sky;and for everything
which is natural which is infinite which is yes

(i who have died am alive again today,
and this is the sun's birthday;this is the birth
day of life and of love and wings:and of the gay
great happening illimitably earth)

how should tasting touching hearing seeing
breathing any—lifted from the no
of all nothing—human merely being
doubt unimaginable You?

(now the ears of my ears awake and
now the eyes of my eyes are opened)

GEOFFREY CHAUCER

Roundel

Now welcome Summer with thy sunnė soft,
That hast this winter's weathers overshake,
And driven away the longė nightės black.

Saint Valentine, that art full high aloft,
Thus singen smallė fowlės for thy sake;
Now welcome Summer with thy sunnė soft,
That hast this winter's weathers overshake.

Well have they causė for to gladden oft,
Since each of them recovered hath his make.
Full blissful may they singė when they wake:
Now welcome Summer with thy sunnė soft,
That hast this winter's weathers overshake,
And driven away the longė nightės black!

WILLIAM HENRY DAVIES

Leisure

What is this life if, full of care,
We have no time to stand and stare.

No time to stand beneath the boughs
And stare as long as sheep or cows.

No time to see, when woods we pass,
Where squirrels hide their nuts in grass.

No time to see, in broad daylight,
Streams full of stars, like skies at night.

No time to turn at Beauty's glance,
And watch her feet, how they can dance.

No time to wait till her mouth can
Enrich that smile her eyes began.

A poor life this if, full of care,
We have no time to stand and stare.

CAROL ANN DUFFY

Talent

This is the word *tightrope*. Now imagine
a man, inching across it in the space
between our thoughts. He holds our breath.

There is no word *net*.

You want him to fall, don't you?
I guessed as much; he teeters but succeeds.
The word *applause* is written all over him.

GEORGE ELIOT

Count That Day Lost

If you sit down at set of sun
And count the acts that you have done,
And, counting, find
One self-denying deed, one word
That eased the heart of him who heard,
One glance most kind
That fell like sunshine where it went –
Then you may count that day well spent.

But if, through all the livelong day,
You've cheered no heart, by yea or nay –
If, through it all
You've nothing done that you can trace
That brought the sunshine to one face –
No act most small
That helped some soul and nothing cost –
Then count that day as worse than lost.

LOUIS MACNEICE

Apple Blossom

The first blossom was the best blossom
For the child who never had seen an orchard;
For the youth whom whisky had led astray
The morning after was the first day.

The first apple was the best apple
For Adam before he heard the sentence;
When the flaming sword endorsed the Fall
The trees were his to plant for all.

The first ocean was the best ocean
For the child from streets of doubt and litter;
For the youth for whom the skies unfurled
His first love was his first world.

But the first verdict seemed the worst verdict
When Adam and Eve were expelled from Eden;
Yet when the bitter gates clanged to
The sky beyond was just as blue.

For the next ocean is the first ocean
And the last ocean is the first ocean
And, however often the sun may rise,
A new thing dawns upon our eyes.

For the last blossom is the first blossom
And the first blossom is the best blossom
And when from Eden we take our way
The morning after is the first day.

CRAIG RAINE

Heaven on Earth

Now that it is night,
you fetch in the washing
from outer space,

from the frozen garden
filmed like a kidney,
with a ghost in your mouth,

and everything you hold,
two floating shirts, a sheet,
ignores the law of gravity.

Only this morning,
the wren at her millinery,
making a baby's soft bonnet,

as we stopped by the spring,
watching the water
well up in the grass,

as if the world were teething.
It was heaven on earth
and it was only the morning.

CHRISTOPHER MARLOWE

The Passionate Shepherd to his Love

Come live with me and be my Love,
And we will all the pleasures prove
That hills and valleys, dale and field,
And all the craggy mountains yield.

There will we sit upon the rocks
And see the shepherds feed their flocks,
By shallow rivers, to whose falls
Melodious birds sing madrigals.

There will I make thee beds of roses
And a thousand fragrant posies,
A cap of flowers, and a kirtle
Embroider'd all with leaves of myrtle.

A gown made of the finest wool,
Which from our pretty lambs we pull,
Fair linèd slippers for the cold,
With buckles of the purest gold.

A belt of straw and ivy buds
With coral clasps and amber studs:
And if these pleasures may thee move,
Come live with me and be my Love.

Thy silver dishes for thy meat
As precious as the gods do eat,
Shall on an ivory table be
Prepared each day for thee and me.

The shepherd swains shall dance and sing
For thy delight each May-morning:
If these delights thy mind may move,
Then live with me and be my Love.

DENISE LEVERTOV

Variation on a Theme by Rilke

The Book of Hours, Book 1, Poem 1, Stanza 1

A certain day became a presence to me;
there it was, confronting me – a sky, air, light:
a being. And before it started to descend
from the height of noon, it leaned over
and struck my shoulder as if with
the flat of a sword, granting me
honor and a task. The day's blow
rang out, metallic or it was I, a bell awakened,
and what I heard was my whole self
saying and singing what it knew: *I can.*

TED HUGHES

Full Moon and Little Frieda

A cool small evening shrunk to a dog bark and the clank of
    a bucket –

And you listening.
A spider's web, tense for the dew's touch.
A pail lifted, still and brimming – mirror
To tempt a first star to a tremor.

Cows are going home in the lane there, looping the hedges
    with their warm wreaths of breath –
A dark river of blood, many boulders,
Balancing unspilled milk.

'Moon!' you cry suddenly, 'Moon! Moon!'

The moon has stepped back like an artist gazing amazed at
    a work

That points at him amazed.

GERARD MANLEY HOPKINS

Spring

Nothing is so beautiful as spring –
   When weeds, in wheels, shoot long and lovely and lush;
   Thrush's eggs look little low heavens, and thrush
Through the echoing timber does so rinse and wring
The ear, it strikes like lightnings to hear him sing;
   The glassy peartree leaves and blooms, they brush
   The descending blue; that blue is all in a rush
With richness; the racing lambs too have fair their fling.

What is all this juice and all this joy?
   A strain of the earth's sweet being in the beginning
In Eden garden. – Have, get, before it cloy,
   Before it cloud, Christ, lord, and sour with sinning,
Innocent mind and Mayday in girl and boy,
   Most, O maid's child, thy choice and worthy the winning.

SEAMUS HEANEY

The Railway Children

When we climbed the slopes of the cutting
We were eye-level with the white cups
Of the telegraph poles and the sizzling wires.

Like lovely freehand they curved for miles
East and miles west beyond us, sagging
Under their burden of swallows.

We were small and thought we knew nothing
Worth knowing. We thought words travelled the wires
In the shiny pouches of raindrops,

Each one seeded full with the light
Of the sky, the gleam of the lines, and ourselves
So infinitesimally scaled

We could stream through the eye of a needle.

The Old World

I believe in the soul; so far
It hasn't made much difference.
I remember an afternoon in Sicily.
The ruins of some temple.
Columns fallen in the grass like naked lovers.

The olives and goat cheese tasted delicious
And so did the wine
With which I toasted the coming night,
The darting swallows,
The Saracen wind and moon.

It got darker. There was something
Long before there were words:
The evening meal of shepherds ...
A fleeting whiteness among the trees ...
Eternity eavesdropping on time.

The goddess going to bathe in the sea.
She must not be followed.
These rocks, these cypress trees,
May be her old lovers.
Oh to be one of them, the wine whispered to me.

JAMES WRIGHT

Lying in a Hammock at William Duffy's Farm in Pine Island, Minnesota

Over my head, I see the bronze butterfly,
Asleep on the black trunk,
Blowing like a leaf in green shadow.
Down the ravine behind the empty house,
The cowbells follow one another
Into the distances of the afternoon.
To my right,
In a field of sunlight between two pines,
The droppings of last year's horses
Blaze up into golden stones.
I lean back as the evening darkens and comes on.
A chicken hawk floats over, looking for home.
I have wasted my life.

You're

Clownlike, happiest on your hands,
Feet to the stars, and moon-skulled,
Gilled like a fish. A common-sense
Thumbs-down on the dodo's mode.
Wrapped up in yourself like a spool,
Trawling your dark as owls do.
Mute as a turnip from the Fourth
Of July to All Fools' Day,
O high-riser, my little loaf.

Vague as fog and looked for like mail.
Farther off than Australia.
Bent-backed Atlas, our travelled prawn.
Snug as a bud and at home
Like a sprat in a pickle jug.
A creel of eels, all ripples.
Jumpy as a Mexican bean.
Right, like a well-done sum.
A clean slate, with your own face on.

ALISON FELL

Pushing Forty

Just before winter
we see the trees show
their true colours:
the mad yellow of chestnuts
two maples like blood sisters
the orange beech
braver than lipstick

Pushing forty, we vow
that when the time comes
rather than wither
ladylike and white
we will henna our hair
like Colette, we too
will be gold and red
and go out
in a last wild blaze

ARTHUR HUGH CLOUGH

Say not the struggle nought availeth,
  The labour and the wounds are vain,
The enemy faints not, nor faileth,
  And as things have been, things remain.

If hopes were dupes, fears may be liars;
  It may be, in yon smoke concealed,
Your comrades chase e'en now the fliers,
  And, but for you, possess the field.

For while the tired waves, vainly breaking,
  Seem here no painful inch to gain,
Far back through creeks and inlets making
  Comes, silent, flooding in, the main,

And not by eastern windows only,
  When daylight comes, comes in the light,
In front the sun climbs slow, how slowly,
  But westward, look, the land is bright.

LOUIS UNTERMEYER

Portrait of a Child

Unconscious of amused and tolerant eyes,
He sits among his scattered dreams, and plays,
True to no one thing long; running for praise
With something less than half begun. He tries
To build his blocks against the furthest skies.
They fall; his soldiers tumble; but he stays
And plans and struts and laughs at fresh dismays,
Too confident and busy to be wise.

His toys are towns and temples; his commands
Bring forth vast armies trembling at his nod.
He shapes and shatters with impartial hands.
And, in his crude and tireless play, I see
The savage, the creator, and the god:
All that man was and all he hopes to be.

JOHN DONNE

The Good Morrow

I wonder, by my troth, what thou and I
   Did, till we loved: were we not weaned till then,
   But sucked on childish pleasures sillily?
   Or slumbered we in th'Seven Sleepers' den?
  'Twas so: but this, all pleasures fancies be.
  If ever any beauty I did see,
Which I desired, and got, 'twas but a dream of thee.

   And now, 'Good morrow' to our waking souls,
   Which watch not one another out of fear,
   But love all love of other sights controls,
   And makes a little room an everywhere.
  Let sea-discov'rers to new worlds have gone;
  Let maps to others, worlds on worlds have shown;
Let us possess our world: each hath one, and is one.

   My face in thine eye, thine in mine appears,
   And plain, true hearts do in the faces rest.
   Where can we find two fitter hemispheres
   Without sharp North, without declining West?
  What ever dies, is not mixed equally:
  If both our loves be one, or thou and I
Love just alike in all, none of these loves can die.

WENDELL BERRY

The Peace of Wild Things

When despair for the world grows in me
and I wake in the night at the least sound
in fear of what my life and my children's lives may be,
I go and lie down where the wood drake
rests in his beauty on the water, and the great heron feeds.
I come into the peace of wild things
who do not tax their lives with forethought
of grief. I come into the presence of still water.
And I feel above me the day-blind stars
waiting with their light. For a time
I rest in the grace of the world, and am free.

DYLAN THOMAS

Do not go gentle into that good night

Do not go gentle into that good night,
Old age should burn and rave at close of day;
Rage, rage against the dying of the light.

Though wise men at their end know dark is right,
Because their words had forked no lightning they
Do not go gentle into that good night.

Good men, the last wave by, crying how bright
Their frail deeds might have danced in a green bay,
Rage, rage against the dying of the light.

Wild men who caught and sang the sun in flight,
And learn, too late, they grieved it on its way,
Do not go gentle into that good night.

Grave men, near death, who see with blinding sight
Blind eyes could blaze like meteors and be gay,
Rage, rage against the dying of the light.

And you, my father, there on the sad height,
Curse, bless, me now with your fierce tears, I pray.
Do not go gentle into that good night.
Rage, rage against the dying of the light.

DOUGLAS DUNN

Modern Love

It is summer, and we are in a house
That is not ours, sitting at a table
Enjoying minutes of a rented silence,
The upstairs people gone. The pigeons lull
To sleep the under-tens and invalids,
The tree shakes out its shadows to the grass,
The roses rove through the wilds of my neglect.
Our lives flap, and we have no hope of better
Happiness than this, not much to show for love
But how we are, or how this evening is,
Unpeopled, silent, and where we are alive
In a domestic love, seemingly alone,
All other lives worn down to trees and sunlight,
Looking forward to a visit from the cat.

JOHN MILTON

On His Blindness

Sonnet XIX

When I consider how my light is spent,
  Ere half my days, in this dark world and wide,
  And that one talent which is death to hide
  Lodged with me useless, though my soul more bent
To serve therewith my Maker, and present
  My true account, lest he returning chide,
  "Doth God exact day-labor, light denied?"
  I fondly ask. But Patience, to prevent
That murmur, soon replies: "God doth not need
  Either man's work or his own gifts; who best
  Bear his mild yoke, they serve him best. His state
Is kingly: thousands at his bidding speed,
  And post o'er land and ocean without rest;
  They also serve who only stand and wait."

OGDEN NASH

Reflections on Ice-Breaking

Candy
is dandy
But liquor
is quicker.

PHILIP LARKIN

Church Going

Once I am sure there's nothing going on
I step inside, letting the door thud shut.
Another church: matting, seats, and stone,
And little books; sprawlings of flowers, cut
For Sunday, brownish now; some brass and stuff
Up at the holy end; the small neat organ;
And a tense, musty, unignorable silence,
Brewed God knows how long. Hatless, I take off
My cycle-clips in awkward reverence,

Move forward, run my hand around the font.
From where I stand, the roof looks almost new –
Cleaned, or restored? Someone would know: I don't.
Mounting the lectern, I peruse a few
Hectoring large-scale verses, and pronounce
'Here endeth' much more loudly than I'd meant.
The echoes snigger briefly. Back at the door
I sign the book, donate an Irish sixpence,
Reflect the place was not worth stopping for.

Yet stop I did: in fact I often do,
And always end much at a loss like this,
Wondering what to look for; wondering, too,
When churches fall completely out of use
What we shall turn them into, if we shall keep
A few cathedrals chronically on show,
Their parchment, plate and pyx in locked cases,
And let the rest rent-free to rain and sheep.
Shall we avoid them as unlucky places?

Or, after dark, will dubious women come
To make their children touch a particular stone;
Pick simples for a cancer; or on some
Advised night see walking a dead one?
Power of some sort or other will go on
In games, in riddles, seemingly at random;
But superstition, like belief, must die,
And what remains when disbelief has gone?
Grass, weedy pavement, brambles, buttress, sky,

A shape less recognisable each week,
A purpose more obscure. I wonder who
Will be the last, the very last, to seek
This place for what it was; one of the crew
That tap and jot and know what rood-lofts were?
Some ruin-bibber, randy for antique,
Or Christmas-addict, counting on a whiff
Of gown-and-bands and organ-pipes and myrrh?
Or will he be my representative,

Bored, uninformed, knowing the ghostly silt
Dispersed, yet tending to this cross of ground
Through suburb scrub because it held unspilt
So long and equably what since is found
Only in separation – marriage, and birth,
And death, and thoughts of these – for which was built
This special shell? For, though I've no idea
What this accoutred frowsty barn is worth,
It pleases me to stand in silence here;

A serious house on serious earth it is,
In whose blent air all our compulsions meet,
Are recognised, and robed as destinies.
And that much never can be obsolete,
Since someone will forever be surprising
A hunger in himself to be more serious,
And gravitating with it to this ground,
Which, he once heard, was proper to grow wise in,
If only that so many dead lie round.

SIMONIDES

For the Spartan Dead at Thermopylai

Tell them in Lakedaimon, passerby
That here, obedient to their laws, we lie.

anonymous translation from the Greek

EMILY BRONTË

The Old Stoic

Riches I hold in light esteem;
    And Love I laugh to scorn;
And lust of fame was but a dream
    That vanished with the morn:

And if I pray, the only prayer
    That moves my lips for me
Is, 'Leave the heart that now I bear,
    And give me liberty!'

Yes, as my swift days near their goal,
    'Tis all that I implore;
In life and death, a chainless soul,
    With courage to endure.

DEREK WALCOTT

Earth

Let the day grow on you upward
through your feet,
the vegetal knuckles,

to your knees of stone,
until by evening you are a black tree;
feel, with evening,

the swifts thicken your hair,
the new moon rising out of your forehead,
and the moonlit veins of silver

running from your armpits
like rivulets under white leaves.
Sleep, as ants

cross over your eyelids.
You have never possessed anything
as deeply as this.

This is all you have owned
from the first outcry
through forever;

you can never be dispossessed.

ROBERT HERRICK

To the Virgins, to Make Much of Time

Gather ye rose-buds while ye may,
    Old Time is still a flying;
And this same flow'r, that smiles to-day,
    To-morrow will be dying.

The glorious lamp of heav'n, the sun,
    The higher he's a getting;
The sooner will his race be run,
    And nearer he's to setting.

That age is best which is the first,
    When youth and blood are warmer;
But, being spent, the worse; and worst
    Times still succeed the former.

Then be not coy, but use your time;
    And while ye may, go marry:
For, having lost but once your prime,
    You may for ever tarry.

GAVIN EWART

June 1966

Lying flat in the bracken of Richmond Park
while the legs and voices of my children pass
seeking, seeking; I remember how on the
13th of June of that simmering 1940
I was conscripted into the East Surreys,
and, more than a quarter of a century
ago, when France had fallen,
we practised concealment in this very bracken.
The burnt stalks pricked through my denims.
Hitler is now one of the antiques of History,
I lurk like a monster in my hiding place.
He didn't get me. If there were a God
it would be only polite to thank him.

Some say that love's a little boy,
     And some say it's a bird,
Some say it makes the world go round,
     And some say that's absurd,
And when I asked the man next-door,
     Who looked as if he knew,
His wife got very cross indeed,
     And said it wouldn't do.

    Does it look like a pair of pyjamas,
     Or the ham in a temperance hotel?
    Does its odour remind one of llamas,
     Or has it a comforting smell?
    Is it prickly to touch as a hedge is,
     Or soft as eiderdown fluff
    Is it sharp or quite smooth at the edges?
     O tell me the truth about love.

Our history books refer to it
     In cryptic little notes,
It's quite a common topic on
     The Transatlantic boats;
I've found the subject mentioned in
     Accounts of suicides,
And even seen it scribbled on
     The backs of railway-guides.

Does it howl like a hungry Alsatian,
　　Or boom like a military band?
Could one give a first-rate imitation
　　On a saw or a Steinway Grand?
Is its singing at parties a riot?
　　Does it only like Classical stuff?
Will it stop when one wants to be quiet?
　　O tell me the truth about love.

I looked inside the summer-house;
　　It wasn't ever there:
I tried the Thames at Maidenhead,
　　And Brighton's bracing air.
I don't know what the blackbird sang,
　　Or what the tulip said;
But it wasn't in the chicken-run,
　　Or underneath the bed.

Can it pull extraordinary faces?
　　Is it usually sick on a swing?
Does it spend all its time at the races,
　　Or fiddling with pieces of string?
Has it views of its own about money?
　　Does it think Patriotism enough?
Are its stories vulgar but funny?
　　O tell me the truth about love.

When it comes, will it come without warning
　　Just as I'm picking my nose?
Will it knock on my door in the morning,
　　Or tread in the bus on my toes?
Will it come like a change in the weather?
　　Will its greeting be courteous or rough?
Will it alter my life altogether?
　　O tell me the truth about love.

SIMON ARMITAGE

The Catch

Forget
the long, smouldering
afternoon. It is

this moment
when the ball scoots
off the edge

of the bat; upwards,
backwards, falling
seemingly

beyond him
yet he reaches
and picks it

out
of its loop
like

an apple
from a branch,
the first of the season.

RAYMOND CARVER

Happiness

So early it's still almost dark out.
I'm near the window with coffee,
and the usual early morning stuff
that passes for thought.
When I see the boy and his friend
walking up the road
to deliver the newspaper.
They wear caps and sweaters,
and one boy has a bag over his shoulder.
They are so happy
they aren't saying anything, these boys.
I think if they could, they would take
each other's arm.
It's early in the morning,
and they are doing this thing together.
They come on, slowly.
The sky is taking on light,
though the moon still hangs pale over the water.
Such beauty that for a minute
death and ambition, even love,
doesn't enter into this.
Happiness. It comes on
unexpectedly. And goes beyond, really,
any early morning talk about it.

PATRICK KAVANAGH

Inniskeen Road: July Evening

The bicycles go by in twos and threes –
There's a dance in Billy Brennan's barn tonight,
And there's the half-talk code of mysteries
And the wink-and-elbow language of delight.
Half-past eight and there is not a spot
Upon a mile of road, no shadow thrown
That might turn out a man or woman, not
A footfall tapping secrecies of stone.

I have what every poet hates in spite
Of all the solemn talk of contemplation.
Oh, Alexander Selkirk knew the plight
Of being king and government and nation.
A road, a mile of kingdom, I am king
Of banks and stones and every blooming thing.

GEORGE GORDON, LORD BYRON

She Walks in Beauty

She walks in beauty, like the night
   Of cloudless climes and starry skies;
And all that's best of dark and bright
   Meet in her aspect and her eyes:
Thus mellow'd to that tender light
   Which heaven to gaudy day denies.

One shade the more, one ray the less,
   Had half impair'd the nameless grace
Which waves in every raven tress,
   Or softly lightens o'er her face;
Where thoughts serenely sweet express
   How pure, how dear their dwelling-place.

And on that cheek, and o'er that brow,
   So soft, so calm, yet eloquent,
The smiles that win, the tints that glow,
   But tell of days in goodness spent,
A mind at peace with all below,
   A heart whose love is innocent!

LANGSTON HUGHES

Dreams

Hold fast to dreams
For if dreams die
Life is a broken-winged bird
That cannot fly.
Hold fast to dreams
For when dreams go
Life is a barren field
Frozen with snow.

D. H. LAWRENCE

Green

The dawn was apple-green,
   The sky was green wine held up in the sun,
The moon was a golden petal between.

She opened her eyes, and green
   They shone, clear like flowers undone
For the first time, now for the first time seen.

CHRISTINA ROSSETTI

A Birthday

My heart is like a singing bird
    Whose nest is in a watered shoot:
My heart is like an apple-tree
    Whose boughs are bent with thickset fruit;
My heart is like a rainbow shell
    That paddles in a halcyon sea;
My heart is gladder than all these
    Because my love is come to me.

Raise me a dais of silk and down:
    Hang it with vair and purple dyes;
Carve it in doves and pomegranates,
    And peacocks with a hundred eyes;
Work it in gold and silver grapes,
    In leaves and silver fleurs-de-lys;
Because the birthday of my life
    Is come, my love is come to me.

MICHAEL DONAGHY

The Present

For the present there is just one moon,
though every level pond gives back another.

But the bright disc shining in the black lagoon,
perceived by astrophysicist and lover,

is milliseconds old. And even that light's
seven minutes older than its source.

And the stars we think we see on moonless nights
are long extinguished. And, of course,

this very moment, as you read this line,
is literally gone before you know it.

Forget the here-and-now. We have no time
but this device of wantoness and wit.

Make me this present then: your hand in mine,
and we'll live out our lives in it.

ANON

What I spent I had,
What I saved I lost,
What I gave I have.

Old German motto

SAMUEL TAYLOR COLERIDGE

Frost at Midnight

The Frost performs its secret ministry,
Unhelped by any wind. The owlet's cry
Came loud – and hark, again! loud as before.
The inmates of my cottage, all at rest,
Have left me to that solitude, which suits
Abstruser musings: save that at my side
My cradled infant slumbers peacefully.
'Tis calm indeed! so calm, that it disturbs
And vexes meditation with its strange
And extreme silentness. Sea, hill, and wood,
This populous village! Sea, and hill, and wood,
With all the numberless goings on of life,
Inaudible as dreams! the thin blue flame
Lies on my low burnt fire, and quivers not;
Only that film, which fluttered on the grate,
Still flutters there, the sole unquiet thing.
Methinks, its motion in this hush of nature
Gives it dim sympathies with me who live,
Making it a companionable form,
Whose puny flaps and freaks the idling Spirit
By its own moods interprets, every where
Echo or mirror seeking of itself,
And makes a toy of Thought.

      But O! how oft,
 How oft, at school, with most believing mind,
Presageful, have I gazed upon the bars,

To watch that fluttering *stranger!* and as oft
With unclosed lids, already had I dreamt
Of my sweet birth-place, and the old church-tower,
Whose bells, the poor man's only music, rang
From morn to evening, all the hot Fair-day,
So sweetly, that they stirred and haunted me
With a wild pleasure, falling on mine ear
Most like articulate sounds of things to come!
So gazed I, till the soothing things, I dreamt,
Lulled me to sleep, and sleep prolonged my dreams!
And so I brooded all the following morn,
Awed by the stern preceptor's face, mine eye
Fixed with mock study on my swimming book:
Save if the door half opened, and I snatched
A hasty glance, and still my heart leaped up,
For still I hoped to see the *stranger's* face,
Townsman, or aunt, or sister more beloved,
My play-mate when we both were clothed alike!

Dear Babe, that sleepest cradled by my side,
Whose gentle breathings, heard in this deep calm,
Fill up the interspersed vacancies
And momentary pauses of the thought!
My babe so beautiful! it thrills my heart
With tender gladness, thus to look at thee,
And think that thou shalt learn far other lore
And in far other scenes! For I was reared
In the great city, pent 'mid cloisters dim,
And saw nought lovely but the sky and stars.
But *thou*, my babe! shalt wander like a breeze
By lakes and sandy shores, beneath the crags
Of ancient mountain, and beneath the clouds,
Which image in their bulk both lakes and shores

And mountain crags: so shalt thou see and hear
The lovely shapes and sounds intelligible
Of that eternal language, which thy God
Utters, who from eternity doth teach
Himself in all, and all things in himself.
Great universal Teacher! he shall mould
Thy spirit, and by giving make it ask.

Therefore all seasons shall be sweet to thee,
Whether the summer clothe the general earth
With greenness, or the redbreast sit and sing
Betwixt the tufts of snow on the bare branch
Of mossy apple-tree, while the nigh thatch
Smokes in the sun-thaw; whether the eve-drops fall
Heard only in the trances of the blast,
Or if the secret ministry of frost
Shall hang them up in silent icicles,
Quietly shining to the quiet Moon.

RAYMOND CARVER

Late Fragment

And did you get what
you wanted from this life, even so?
I did.
And what did you want?
To call myself beloved, to feel myself
beloved on the earth.

T. S. ELIOT

from Little Gidding

V

What we call the beginning is often the end
And to make an end is to make a beginning.
The end is where we start from. And every phrase
And sentence that is right (where every word is at home,
Taking its place to support the others,
The word neither diffident nor ostentatious,
An easy commerce of the old and the new,
The common word exact without vulgarity,
The formal word precise but not pedantic,
The complete consort dancing together)
Every phrase and every sentence is an end and a beginning,
Every poem an epitaph. And any action
Is a step to the block, to the fire, down the sea's throat
Or to an illegible stone: and that is where we start.
We die with the dying:
See, they depart, and we go with them.
We are born with the dead:
See, they return, and bring us with them.
The moment of the rose and the moment of the yew-tree
Are of equal duration. A people without history
Is not redeemed from time, for history is a pattern
Of timeless moments. So, while the light fails
On a winter's afternoon, in a secluded chapel
History is now and England.

With the drawing of this Love and the voice of this Calling
We shall not cease from exploration
And the end of all our exploring
Will be to arrive where we started
And know the place for the first time.
Through the unknown, remembered gate
When the last of earth left to discover
Is that which was the beginning;
At the source of the longest river
The voice of the hidden waterfall
And the children in the apple-tree
Not known, because not looked for
But heard, half-heard, in the stillness
Between two waves of the sea.
Quick now, here, now, always –
A condition of complete simplicity
(Costing not less than everything)
And all shall be well and
All manner of thing shall be well
When the tongues of flame are in-folded
Into the crowned knot of fire
And the fire and the rose are one.

ACKNOWLEDGEMENTS

The editor and publishers gratefully acknowledge permission to reprint copyright material in this book as follows:

ANNA AKHMATOVA: 'Our Own Land' © Anna Akhmatova from *Selected Poems* by kind permission of Richard McKane and Bloodaxe Books.

MAYA ANGELOU: 'Still I Rise' © 1978 by Maya Angelou, from *And Still I Rise* by Maya Angelou, and 'Caged Bird' © 1983 by Maya Angelou, from *Shaker, Why Don't You Sing?* by Maya Angelou. Used by permission of Random House, Inc.

SIMON ARMITAGE: 'Let Me Put it This Way' taken from *Book of Matches* and 'The Catch' taken from *Kid* © Simon Armitage and reprinted by kind permission of Faber and Faber Ltd.

EDMUND BLUNDEN: 'Report on Experience' from Edmund Blunden: *Selected Poems* (Carcanet) by kind permission of the Estate of Edmund Blunden.

PAT BORAN: 'Waving' © Pat Boran, from *Familiar Things* (1993). With permission of Dedalus Press, Dublin, Ireland, www.dedaluspress.com.

COLETTE BRYCE: 'Early Version' © by kind permission of the poet and Macmillan Publishers Ltd.

RAYMOND CARVER: 'Happiness' from *Where Water Comes Together with Other Water* by Raymond Carver, © 1984, 1985 by Raymond Carver. Used by permission of Random House, Inc.

CHARLES CAUSLEY: 'I Am the Song' from *I Had a Little Cat* by Charles Causley (Macmillan) by kind permission of the Estate of Charles Causley.

INDEX OF POETS

Akhmatova, Anna (1889–1966) 13

Angelou, Maya (b.1928) 8, 125

Anon 3, 130, 191

Archilochus (c.680–c.645 BC) 57

Armitage, Simon (b.1963) 114, 183

Arnold, Matthew (1822–88) 127

Auden, W. H. (1907–73) 132, 181

Berry, Wendell (b.1934) 168

Betjeman, John (1906–84) 56

Bishop, Elizabeth (1911–79) 75

Blake, William (1757–1827) 27, 51, 60, 131

Blunden, Edmund (1896–1974) 70

Bly, Robert (b.1926) 64

Boran, Pat (b.1963) 34

Bradstreet, Anne (1612–72) 137

Brontë, Emily (1818–48) 177

Brooke, Rupert (1887–1915) 36

Browning, Elizabeth Barrett (1806–61) 65

Browning, Robert (1812–89) 30, 54

Bryce, Colette (b.1970) 110

Burns, Robert (1759–96) 38

Burnside, John (b. 1955) 23

Byron, George Gordon, Lord (1788–1824) 186

Callimachus (c.300–240 BC) 28

Carver, Raymond (1938–88) 184, 195

Causley, Charles (1917–2003) 107

Chaucer, Geoffrey (c.1343–1400) 149

Clare, John (1793–1864) 135

Clough, Arthur Hugh (1819–61) 165

Coleridge, Samuel Taylor (1772–1834) 192

Coolidge, Susan (1835–1905) 19

Cope, Wendy (b.1945) 37, 93

Cummings, E. E. (1894–1962) 148

Davies, William Henry (1871–1940) 150

Dickinson, Emily (1830–86) 69

Donaghy, Michael (1954–2004) 40, 190

Donne, John (1572–1631) 20, 167

Dooley, Maura (b.1957) 103

Dryden, John (1631–1700) 94

Duffy, Carol Ann (b.1955) 151

Dunn, Douglas (b.1942) 170

Dunn, Stephen (b.1939) 59

Eliot, George (1819–80) 152

Eliot, T. S. (1885–1965) 42, 196

Ewart, Gavin (1916–95) 180

Fanthorpe, U. A. (1929–2009) 129

Farjeon, Eleanor (1881–1965) 21

Fell, Alison (b.1944) 164

Fenton, James (b.1949) 29

Frost, Robert (1874–1963) 68, 109

Frye, Mary E. (1905–2004) 124

Graves, Robert (1895–1985) 88

Gunn, Thom (1929–2004) 18

Hafez (1325–90) 42

Hammerstein II, Oscar (1895–1960) 15

Hanagid, Shmuel (993–1056) 96

Hardy, Thomas (1840–1928) 77

Heaney, Seamus (b.1939) 11, 91, 160

Henley, William Ernest (1849–1903) 58

Herbert, George (1593–1633) 90
Herrick, Robert (1591–1674) 32,
 99, 179
Hopkins, Gerard Manley (1844–89)
 10, 159
Housman, A. E. (1859–1936) 92
Hughes, Langston (1902–67) 97,
 187
Hughes, Ted (1930–98) 158
Jamie, Kathleen (b.1962) 108
Kavanagh, Patrick (1904–67) 185
Kay, Jackie (b.1961) 140
Keats, John (1795–1821) 5, 98
The King James Bible (1611) 16
Kipling, Rudyard (1865–1936) 104
Larkin, Philip (1922–85) 142, 173
Lawrence, D. H. (1885–1930) 188
Levertov, Denise (1923–97) 157
Logue, Christopher (1926–2011) 6
Lowell, Amy (1874–1925) 99
McGough, Roger (b.1937) 122
MacNeice, Louis (1907–63) 153
Magee, John Gillespie (1922–41) 7
Mahon, Derek (b.1941) 143
de la Mare, Walter (1873–1956) 118
Marlowe, Christopher (1564–95)
 41, 155
Marvell, Andrew (1621–78) 141
Masefield, John (1878–1967) 76
Milne, A. A. (1882–1956) 17
Milton, John (1608–74) 171
Mitchell, Adrian (1932–2008) 61
Moore, Marianne (1887–1972) 102
Nash, Ogden (1902–71) 172
Neruda, Pablo (1904–73) 138
Niemöller, Pastor (1892–1984) 106
O'Brien, Sean (b.1952) 52
Oswald, Alice (b.1966) 87
Parker, Dorothy (1893–1967) 86

Paterson, Don (b.1963) 67
Plath, Sylvia (1932–63) 163
Pollard, Clare (b.1978) 80
Pugh, Sheenagh (b.1950) 4, 116
Raine, Craig (b.1944) 154
Roethke, Theodore (1908–63) 62
Rossetti, Christina (1830–94) 50,
 72, 189
Rumi, Jalaluddin (1207–73) 121
Sansom, Ann (b.1951) 31
Sassoon, Siegfried (1886–1967) 95
Shakespeare, William (1564–1616)
 22, 78, 101
Shelley, Percy Bysshe (1792–1822)
 144
Simic, Charles (b.1938) 161
Simonides (*c.*556–469 BC) 176
Smith, Stevie (1902–71) 71
Tennyson, Alfred, Lord (1809–92)
 14, 111
Thomas, Dylan (1914–53) 55, 169
Thomas, Edward (1878–1917) 145
Tolkien, J. R. R. (1892–1973) 74
Untermeyer, Louis (1885–1977) 166
da Vinci, Leonardo (1452–1519) 120
Walcott, Derek (b.1930) 178
Whitman, Walt (1819–92) 119
Wilcox, Ella Wheeler (1850–1919)
 85
Williams, William Carlos
 (1883–1963) 33
Wintle, Walter D. (late C19–C20
 centuries) 49
Wordsworth, William (1770–1850)
 12, 66, 136
Wotton, Sir Henry (1568–1639)
 146
Wright, James (1927–80) 162
Yeats, W. B. (1865–1939) 26, 63, 115

INDEX OF TITLES AND FIRST LINES

a burst of iris so that 33

A certain day became a presence to me 157

A cool small evening shrunk to a dog bark and the clank of a bucket 158

A state you must dare not enter 59

A thing of beauty is a joy for ever 5

Adlestrop 145

Afterwards 77

All that is gold does not glitter 74

All winter I was waiting 140

And death shall have no dominion 55

And did those feet in ancient time 60

And did you get what 195

Apple Blossom 153

As a child I waved to people I didn't know 34

As I walked out one evening 132

Atlas 129

Auguries of Innocence 51

Auld Lang Syne 38

Be cheerful, sir 22

Being 67

Being Boring 37

A Birthday 189

Call, by all means, but just once 31

Candy 172

The Catch 183

Celia Celia 61

The Character of a Happy Life 146

The Charge of the Light Brigade 111

Children, if you dare to think 88

A Christmas Carol 72

Church Going 173

Climbing 100

Clownlike, happiest on your hands 163

Come, come, for you will not find another friend like Me 121

Come live with me and be my Love 155

Come to the Edge 6

Conquer we shall, but we must first contend 99

Conviction 71

Count That Day Lost 152

The Daffodils 136

Dead Woman 138

Dearest, note how these two are alike 40

Devotions Upon Emergent Occasions 20

Dignified 52

Do not go gentle into that good Night 169

Do not stand at my grave and weep 124

Does the road wind up-hill all the way? 50

Don't see him. Don't phone or write a letter 93

Dover Beach 127

Dreams 187
Dusk-light; the news tells of
    another train derailed 80

Early Version 110
Earth 178
Earth has not anything to show
    more fair 12
The End (Milne) 17
The End (Herrick) 99
Endymion 5
Envying Owen Beattie 116
An Epilogue 76
Eternity 27
Every day is a fresh beginning 19
Everyone Sang 95
Everyone suddenly burst out
    singing 95
Everything is Going to Be All Right
    143

Fare Well 118
First they came for the Jews 106
For the present there is just one
    moon 190
For the Spartan Dead at Thermopylai
    176
Forget 183
Freight 103
From time to time our love is like
    a sail 87
Frost at Midnight 192
Full Moon and Little Frieda 158

Gather ye rose-buds while ye
    may 179
Give me a man that is not dull 32
Glory be to God for dappled
    things 10

The Good Morrow 167
Green 188

Had I the heavens' embroidered
    cloths 63
Half a league, half a league 111
Happiness (Dunn) 59
Happiness (Carver) 184
Happy the Man 94
Happy the man, and happy he
    alone 94
He turns not back who is bound to
    a star 120
He who binds to himself a joy 27
*He Wishes for the Cloths of
    Heaven* 63
Heaven on Earth 154
Henry V 78
Heraclitus 28
High Flight (An Airman's Ecstasy) 7
High up in the apple tree climbing
    I go 100
Hinterhof 29
His Desire 32
History 23
Hold fast to dreams 187
Holy Island 140
Home-Thoughts, from Abroad 30
How do I love thee? Let me count
    the ways 65
How happy is he born and
    taught 146
How should I not be glad to
    contemplate 143
How straight it flew, how long it
    flew 56
How strange to think of giving up
    all ambition! 64
The Hug 18

'I Am' 135

I am the ship in which you sail 103

I Am the Song 107

I am the song that sings the bird 107

I am – yet what I am none cares or knows 135

I believe in the soul; so far 161

I envy not in any moods 14

I have been young, and now am not too old 70

I have seen flowers come in stony places 76

I know that I shall meet my fate 115

I Know Why the Caged Bird Sings 125

I like to get off with people 71

I May, I Might, I Must 102

I saw a Peacock with a fiery tail 3

i thank You God for most this amazing 148

I, Too 97

I, too, sing America 97

I wake to sleep, and take my waking slow 62

I wander'd lonely as a cloud 136

I went out to the hazel wood 26

I wish I could show you 42

I wonder, by my troth, what thou and I 167

If – 104

If ever two were one, then surely we 137

If I can stop one Heart from breaking 69

If I should die, think only this of me 36

If suddenly you do not exist 138

If you ask me 'What's new?', I have nothing to say 37

If you can keep your head when all about you 104

If you sit down at set of sun 152

If you think you are beaten, you are 49

If you will tell me why the fen 102

In Memoriam A. H. H. 14

In summer's heat, and mid-time of the day 41

In the bleak mid-winter 72

In the pathways of the sun 86

Inniskeen Road: July Evening 185

Invictus 58

Iris 33

An Irish Airman Foresees His Death 115

It is summer, and we are in a house 170

It was your birthday, we had drunk and dined 18

June 1966 180

Just before winter 164

Late Fragment 195

Laugh, and the world laughs with you 85

Leisure 150

Let me put it this way 114

Let the day grow on you upward 178

Let us go then, you and I 43

Life's Variety 130

Little Gidding 196

The Love Song of J. Alfred Prufrock 42

Loveliest of trees, the cherry
  now 92
Lying flat in the bracken of
  Richmond Park 180
*Lying in a Hammock at William
  Duffy's Farm in Pine Island,
  Minnesota* 162

Machines 40
Markings 91
Milton 60
Modern Love 170
Morning has broken 21
Much have I travell'd in the realms
  of gold 98
My beloved spake, and said unto
  me, Rise up 16
My Brilliant Image 42
My heart is like a singing bird 189
My Heart Leaps Up 66
My heart leaps up when I behold
  66

New Every Morning 19
No Man is an Island, entire of it
  self 20
No, the candle is not crying, it
  cannot feel pain 122
Nothing is so beautiful as
  spring 159
Now that it is night 154
Now welcome Summer with thy
  sunne' soft 149

Oh, I have slipped the surly bonds
  of earth 7
Oh, to be in England 30
The Old Stoic 177
The Old World 161

*On First Looking into Chapman's
  Homer* 98
On grim estates at dawn, on college
  tracks 52
On His Blindness 171
Once I am sure there's nothing
  going on 173
Once more unto the breach, dear
  friends, once more 78
One Art 75
Our boat was slow to reach
  Bethsaida; winds oppressed
  us 110
Our Own Land 13
Out of the night that covers me 58
Over my head, I see the bronze
  butterfly 162
Ovid's Elegies 41

Pass the tambourine, let me bash
  our praises 108
The Passionate Shepherd to his Love
  155
The Peace of Wild Things 168
Penelope 86
The Peninsula 11
Pied Beauty 10
Pippa's Song 54
Portrait of a Child 166
Prayer 90
Prayer the Churches banquet,
  Angels age 90
The Present 190
Prometheus Unbound 144
Pushing Forty 164

The Railway Children 160
Reflections on Ice-Breaking 172
Report on Experience 70

Richard II 101
Riches I hold in light esteem 177
Riders 109
The Road Not Taken 68
Roundel 149

Say not the struggle nought availeth 165
Seaside Golf 56
She Walks in Beauty 186
She walks in beauty, like the night 186
Should auld acquaintance be forgot 38
A Shropshire Lad 92
Silent comrade of the distances 67
So early it's still almost dark out 184
Soar, Don't Settle 96
Soar, don't settle for earth 96
The Soldier 36
Solitude 85
Some Saian sports my splendid shield 57
Some say that love's a little boy 181
Sometimes 4
Sometimes things don't go, after all 4
The Song of Solomon 16
The Song of Wandering Aengus 26
Sonnets from the Portuguese 65
Spring 159
Stay near to me and I'll stay near to you 29
Still I Rise 8

Talent 151
Tell them in Lakedaimon, passerby 176

The Tempest 22
The Angel that presided o'er my birth 131
The art of losing isn't hard to master 75
The bicycles go by in twos and threes 185
The dawn was apple-green 188
The first blossom was the best blossom 153
The free bird leaps 125
The Frost performs its secret ministry 192
The sea is calm to-night 127
The surest thing there is is we are riders 109
The trees are coming into leaf 142
The year's at the spring 54
There is a kind of love called maintenance 129
They told me, Heraclitus, they told me you were dead 28
Thinking 49
Thinking of England 80
This is the word tightrope. Now imagine 151
This royal throne of kings, this sceptered isle 101
Thoughts in a Garden 141
To have stood on the Arctic island 116
To my Dear and Loving Husband 137
To see a World in a Grain of Sand 51
To suffer woes which Hope thinks infinite 144
To the Virgins, to Make Much of Time 179
Today 23

The Trees 142
Two Cures for Love 93
Two roads diverged in a yellow
    wood 68

Unconscious of amused and
    tolerant eyes 166
Up-Hill 50
Upon Westminster Bridge 12

Variation on a Theme by Rilke 157
Voice 31

The Waking 62
Walk on, through the wind 15
Warning to Children 88
Watering the Horse 64
Waving 34
The Way Things Are 122
The Way We Live 108
We don't wear it in sacred amulets
    on our chests 13
We marked the pitch: four jackets
    for four goalposts 91
We Two Boys Together Clinging 119
Wedding 87
What I spent I had 191
What If This Road 153
What if this road, that has held no
    surprises 153

What is this life if, full of care
    150
What we call the beginning is
    often the end 196
What wondrous life is this I
    lead! 141
When despair for the world grows
    in me 168
When I am sad and weary 61
When I consider how my light is
    spent 171
When I lie where shades of
    darkness 118
When I was One 17
When the Present has latched its
    postern behind my tremulous
    stay 77
When we climbed the slopes of
    the cutting 160
When you have nothing more to
    say, just drive 11
Why do we grumble because a
    tree is bent 130

Yes. I remember Adlestrop 145
You may write me down in
    history 8
You'll Never Walk Alone 15
You're 163